Francisco Márcio Santos Da Silva

Educational software for automotive electrical circuits

Francisco Márcio Santos Da Silva

Educational software for automotive electrical circuits

Educational software - ELETROAUTOS

ScienciaScripts

Imprint

Any brand names and product names mentioned in this book are subject to trademark, brand or patent protection and are trademarks or registered trademarks of their respective holders. The use of brand names, product names, common names, trade names, product descriptions etc. even without a particular marking in this work is in no way to be construed to mean that such names may be regarded as unrestricted in respect of trademark and brand protection legislation and could thus be used by anyone.

Cover image: www.ingimage.com

This book is a translation from the original published under ISBN 978-3-330-76629-7.

Publisher:
Sciencia Scripts
is a trademark of
Dodo Books Indian Ocean Ltd. and OmniScriptum S.R.L publishing group

120 High Road, East Finchley, London, N2 9ED, United Kingdom
Str. Armeneasca 28/1, office 1, Chisinau MD-2012, Republic of Moldova, Europe
Managing Directors: Ieva Konstantinova, Victoria Ursu
info@omniscriptum.com

ISBN: 978-620-8-54048-7

To God,
Lord of my life
My Saviour in whom I trust. To my mother, Juvenilia,
for her courage and determination. To my father,
Raimundo, a fighter and encourager, who took part in
this stage of my life.

ACKNOWLEDGEMENTS

I thank God for my health, my disposition and his marvellous grace in my life.

I would like to thank my family and my parents, Raimundo Nonato da Silva and Juvenilia Santos da Silva, who have always supported me throughout my life.

I would like to thank SENAI, which has always been a part of my life and to which I am proud to belong.

I would like to thank the MPCOM Master's professors for their dedication, especially my advisor Professor Elian Machado and Professor Willys, who honoured me with his presence at the defence panel; Professor Gilvanise, who demonstrates her love and dedication to education, and the illustrious Professor José Julião, for his contribution to this work.

I would like to thank the coordinator of MPCOMP, Professor Marcos Negreiros, for whom I have great admiration, a dedicated man.

I would like to thank the brothers and sisters of the Lamb Baptist Church, who pray to God for me.

To the students of class T10, who were part of this process with unity and enthusiasm.

SUMMARY

This study aims to develop the ELETROAUTOS Software as an auxiliary tool for teaching automotive electrical circuits, commenting on the stages of development and implementation of the educational software and presenting the pedagogical principles that defined the aspects of its functional architecture. Considering that this educational tool will preferably be used in vocational apprenticeship and qualification courses, subject to the curricular parameters of current Brazilian vocational education, the scenario arising from the use of new educational technologies, based on the use of computers, its implications for the teaching-learning process and the new precepts of the reform of Brazilian vocational education are analysed. The methodology developed in the work follows the precepts of a bibliographical survey that is divided into two stages: the first consists of a literature review pertinent to the topic; the second consists of the development of the software and its evaluation by students and teachers. The results show that the software was satisfactorily evaluated in terms of pedagogical criteria. The experimental activities developed in the virtual environment are linked to the traditional laboratory model through simulation supervised by the teachers taking part in this process.

Keywords: Informatics in Education; Educational Software; Vocational Courses.

SUMMARY

CHAPTER 1

INTRODUCTION

The dealership is the company that represents vehicle manufacturers and operates in the market by selling and offering technical maintenance support and providing corrective and preventive maintenance repair services. Delgado and Kureski (2010), analysing the vehicle repair services market, found that this sector has been restructured in recent decades as a result of advances in the field of microelectronics. These advances have prompted the development of short or long-term training programmes based on technologies involving electricity.

Changes in production models and advances in automotive technology have led to vehicles with complex technology being more in need of specialised labour in the car maintenance market. Electricity and electronics are examples of technologies that are increasingly present in a complex way in motor vehicles. These changes brought about by the insertion of new technologies in cars have had a direct impact on vocational training in automotive maintenance. The schools' reflections have resulted in accompanying teaching techniques, adapting an efficient way of teaching this technology in a simpler language and preparing a workforce suited to the new demands of the market, capable of facing these new challenges in vehicle maintenance.

Among the many learning problems that exist in the field of automotive maintenance, the difficulty of learning electricity and car electrical circuits can be considered a very worrying issue for teachers of vocational courses and automotive maintenance technicians who are looking into the matter and seeking alternatives to alleviate the problem.

When teaching electricity in vocational training courses, students find it difficult to interpret electrical diagrams. This is seen by the teachers at the end of the training course through the final assessments; they realise that many of them have not managed to achieve the desired knowledge expectations from the course. This is worrying, as it is a very significant knowledge base for training and, without it, it is difficult to understand other knowledge that is interconnected with automotive electricity, jeopardising future professionals in the field of vehicle electrical diagnostics.

Vocational training in automobiles needs teaching resources that develop the experimental activities needed to practise the profession of automobile electrical mechanic. In order to improve the efficiency of teaching vehicle electrical content, there is a need for autonomous and collaborative activities during the teaching and learning process. Pereira (2006) states that the principle of flexibility presupposes that the student is seen as an active subject, treated as the protagonist of the training process.

Some educational software has been created in the training centres of car manufacturers with the aim of making it easier for people to learn.

students in the subject of automotive electricity. Software such as Renault S/A's F2K and MWM's Basic Electricity are just a few examples of computer-mediated learning objects that can be used in automotive electrical classes to reduce the cognitive burden of learning. Another important work is that of the company Edisonlab, which provides proprietary software with a virtual laboratory for building electrical circuits. The Portal do Professor repository also offers programmes such as *Farady's and* experiential physics, which could very well be applied to automotive electrical courses.

The development of new teaching resources, such as educational software and virtual learning environments, deserves attention from educators, especially in a society that is evolving in the use of computers.

Applying a tool that favours the learning of students on the automotive electrical course will clarify many questions about the difficulties of learning electrical circuits and encourage students to continue studying new subjects related to automotive electrical and electronic maintenance, contributing, above all, to the quality of their training.

The general aim of this work is to develop educational software for automotive electrical circuits, with a virtual environment for building electrical circuits, with the aim of applying this didactic resource to vocational courses in automotive electricity in the classroom teaching modality.

The methodological procedures included bibliographical research, a review of the literature, followed by the construction and application of the ELETROAUTOS software. The bibliographical research provided information on the subject by reading published articles and books.

In preparing this work, we established the pedagogical aspects that guided the development of educational software and the requirements structured and regulated in its architecture. A pedagogical method was defined for the software's handling and navigation interface, choosing the computer configurations for the educational software's desired architecture.

This work is structured in sections that we will see below.

Section 2 contains a review of the literature and laws regulating vocational education, IT and vocational schools in the automotive sector.

Section 3 deals with educational software and the types of software used in automotive electricity

Section 4 deals with the methodology used to build the ELETROAUTOS software, involving the method used, the stages in the development of the software and the distribution and initial tests with electricity classes from the National Technical Education Programme.

The results and discussions are presented in section 5, which analyses the LO (Learning Object), which is nothing more than the ELETROAUTOS software.

Finally, the concluding remarks outline the conclusions drawn from the results of employee performance, in the light of the assumptions described in the research literature.

CHAPTER 2

PROFESSIONAL EDUCATION AND INFORMATION TECHNOLOGY

Education is the guiding principle for social relations and progress towards a sustainable and healthy society. The Brazilian Education Guidelines and Bases Law (LDB) supports the idea that education encompasses the formative processes that develop in the family, in social coexistence, at work, in educational and research institutions and other social manifestations.

In the context of labour and production, education is an essential process for the development of productivity and technological progress and the constant alignment of innovations, as in the case of information technology, the insertion of the computer and the impacts on this new process.

Law 11.741[1] of 2008 amended provisions in the legislation on guidelines and bases and integrates actions in technical professional education at secondary level. Professional and technological education is integrated with the different levels and modalities of education and with the dimensions of labour, science and technology. In this change, the government's concern with targeting professional and technological education at young people and adults was evident. The law registers the existence of various types of professional education, including apprenticeships, professional qualifications and technical education.

The shortage of qualified labour in the job market is a reality in various segments of production in Brazil. The world of work demands people with the skills and competences to deal with challenging events every day, especially in areas with complex technologies, such as the automotive sector. Nascimento and Araújo (2010) show that changes in vocational training require transformations in the world of work, such as information technology in the production environment. Vocational education is therefore considered a strategic development factor.

In automotive repair, these challenges are constant due to the amount of information and technology available in cars.

The qualification of people in technological training is fundamental for the job market, and the secret is the partnership that vocational training centres have with large local companies that look to them for skilled labour.

2.1 Modalities of Vocational Education

For teaching and learning processes in vocational training, there are modalities regulated by law and developed by the Ministry of Education. Qualifications, apprenticeships and technical courses are very different types of training that cater for different student profiles.

With regard to vocational training and the educational establishment that will develop the actions of

---

[1] The National Programme for Access to Technical Education and Employment (Pronatec) was created by the Federal Government in 2011 with the aim of expanding the supply of professional and technological education courses.

vocational education, the LDB clarifies many of these issues. The law states that general preparation for work and, optionally, vocational training can be developed in secondary schools themselves with specialised vocational education institutions.

SENAI is an educational establishment with a focus on vocational education, specialising in vocational training for industry (automotive manufacturers), which operates in the following teaching modalities: Industrial Apprenticeship, Professional Qualification and Technical Courses.

2.1.1 Industrial Apprenticeship

Law 11.741/2008 amends the LDB and makes a comment on vocational training modalities, stating that vocational and technological education, in fulfilment of the objectives of national education, is integrated with the different levels and modalities of education and with the dimensions of work, science and technology for initial and continuing training or professional qualification.

The automotive maintenance apprenticeship course is a type of continuing training governed by law 10.097/2000, which supports the training of apprentices, and complemented by law 11.741, which ensures free training for young apprentices up to the age of 24. The employment contract for minors or young apprentices is a term that obliges companies, such as dealerships, to hire and train the student to provide services in the company and study at a school regulated for this modality, as expressed in the following quote:

> An apprenticeship contract is a special employment contract, agreed in writing and for a fixed term, in which the employer undertakes to ensure that those over 14 (fourteen) and under 24 (twenty-four) years of age enrolled in an apprenticeship programme receive methodical technical and professional training, compatible with their physical, moral and psychological development, and that the apprentice performs the tasks necessary for this training with zeal and diligence (BRASIL Law 11.741/Art 428).

The automotive repair apprenticeship has a course load of 1,200 hours, when the student does their vocational training at school and their apprenticeship at the company. In the school phase, they study all the mechanical, electrical and electronic systems of the car, defined in a curriculum focussed on vehicle maintenance. Oliveira and Simão (2012) define the idea that "The tasks carried out by minors should be those carried out in the very environment in which they were hired, in tasks of progressive complexity".

Companies are obliged to take on apprentices and, in the case of car dealerships, they are responsible for selecting these young people to work in vehicle maintenance.

2.1.2 Professional Qualification

Another type of education is professional qualification, also governed by Law 11.741. The main characteristic of this type of training, which differentiates it from apprenticeships, is the fragmentation of training with a shorter workload, the special courses.

> Professional and technological education institutions, in addition to their regular courses,

Professional qualification follows a minimum course load of 160 hours, with both theory and practical training. In automotive maintenance training, these courses are offered as initial and continuing training, following a curriculum matrix (figure 2.1) defined by the sectoral technical committee[2] in which the student starts with the initial courses and the sequential courses with defined workloads, respectively.

MODULES	NAME	CURRICULAR UNITS	LOAD HOURS	MODULE WORKLOAD
Basic	Basic	- Organisation of Work environment	30h	oooh
		- Fundamentals of Automotive Technology	30h	
Introductory 1	Introduction to Electro-electronics	- Systems Fundamentals Automotive Electrical	40h	600h
		- Systems Fundamentals Automotive Electronics	20h	
Specific 1	Electricity	- Charging and starting system	60h	lOOh
	Automotive	- Signalling and	40h	

Figure 2.1 - Curriculum matrix - Source: CNI-SENAI.

The National Programme for Access to Technical Education and Employment (PRONATEC) is an example of how the professional qualification modality is used to train public school students free of charge. Law 12.513 of 2011 (BRASIL, 2012) defines that one of the objectives is to expand, internalise and democratise the offer of technical professional education courses at secondary level, in person and at a distance, as well as initial and continuing training courses and programmes or professional qualifications.

Vocational retraining is also a form of qualification, and mechanics who are still in the labour market come to SENAI with the aim of finding new technological information. Many of them are simply looking for innovations in the automotive field, particularly in matters related to electricity, something that many professionals turn to because of the strong presence of this technology in vehicles.

2.2 Vocational Education and Automotive Electrical Maintenance.

The car industry is trying to win over and keep its customers by building attractive vehicles with technological innovation. In Brazil, according to the National Association of Motor Vehicle Manufacturers (ANFAVEA, 2010), there has been a significant increase in interest in vehicles in recent years, especially "flexfuel" technology, which is called an electronic injection system with technology based on electricity and electronics with on-board computers.

In 2008, 2,254,553 units of vehicles with "flexfuel" electronic technology were produced. In 2009, there was a jump in sales of approximately 10%, totalling 2,543,499 units. In 2010, 2,625,092 were produced

---

[2] Sectoral technical committee - These are industrial companies from the automotive sector and Senai have developed a training programme for the Brazilian market.

(ANFAVEA, 2010). In view of the data mentioned, there is a need to train young people and adults to meet the demand for vehicles with electric-based technology.

It is necessary to train professionals, whether in the form of qualifications and apprenticeships or otherwise, on the understanding that the labour market needs a more specialised workforce in automotive electricity, in which the professional carries out routine maintenance activities with autonomy in decision-making, facing up to the challenges of the automotive sector.

In vehicle electrical and electronic systems, there has been an increase in technological innovations in cars. As a result, maintenance of these systems is also growing, and schools must provide professionals who are prepared to deal with these technologies. In order for them to better understand the new technologies that are being introduced into cars, qualification and re-qualification courses are essential.

2.3 IT in Vocational Training

Information technology is another segment on the rise in society, influencing practically all educational modalities. Tablets, notebooks, smartphones and mobile phones, mobile devices and applications are expanding in the consumer market. Mobile computing is also a concrete fact of the new information and communication technology. One example is in cars, with multimedia kits, and in mechanical workshops, with electrical and electronic system diagnostic programmes.

Teaching in vocational training acts on the aspects of reproducing the resources and knowledge of the world of work, bringing the reality of companies into vocational training. Combining qualification and IT in the automotive area will develop skills and knowledge so that students can carry out their professional activities within the technological and structural reality of the automotive industry.

In the industrial and commercial world, computers are an important support tool, influencing productivity. In automotive maintenance, the computer cannot be excluded, and mechanics must adapt by training and adapting to this new structure. In fact, this is one of the missions of professional education in electrical maintenance: to train future professionals to adapt to existing computer resources, in this case the computer and mobile devices, thus improving maintenance diagnoses.

The barriers of sensory, physical and mental disabilities and a low level of schooling are also a major obstacle to the full use of computers in the automotive sector. Many maintenance professionals are not literate enough to use a large part of the content and computer interfaces available today autonomously and skilfully.

In the automotive repair market, the computer is used as a diagnostic tool to solve many electrical problems. The car is a technological product and professionals must have equipment in line with these innovations. Just knowing how to use a computer is not enough: you need to know more about software and its applications, hardware for interacting with the programmes inserted into the car via on-board computers and the whole set becomes indispensable for carrying out a diagnostic and repair task.

2.3.1 Traditional Teaching Resources Used to Teach Automotive Electricity

Every teaching and learning process requires reflection and change, with the aim of proposing the best form of transmission. Traditional teaching methods are still widely used by teachers. Innovations and teaching techniques using computers and educational software have yet to be assimilated by teachers, most of whom use very traditional methods. Weber and Behrens (2010) make an observation about the traditionalism and conservatism of many classroom teachers who resist new teaching and learning practices.

The blackboard and the marker brush are the teacher's inseparable resources, which they use for notes, drawings, electrical diagrams and calculations. Excessive use of any one resource makes the lesson monotonous.

When teaching electrical circuits, it is very common for the teacher to draw electrical diagrams of car circuits on the blackboard and explain them to the students. When constructing circuits on the board, a lot of class time is wasted drawing, which is not an efficient method, as some students find it difficult to understand and try to decipher the graphs and symbols that are pertinent to electrical circuits.

Another outdated resource that is still used in the classroom on car electrical courses is the overhead projector (figure 2.2). This resource is used by the teacher to show content and electrical diagrams. Some teachers use it excessively, projecting their own printed handouts, which can make the work tiring because the projection slides contain a fixed format for the drawings, making the lesson even more boring.

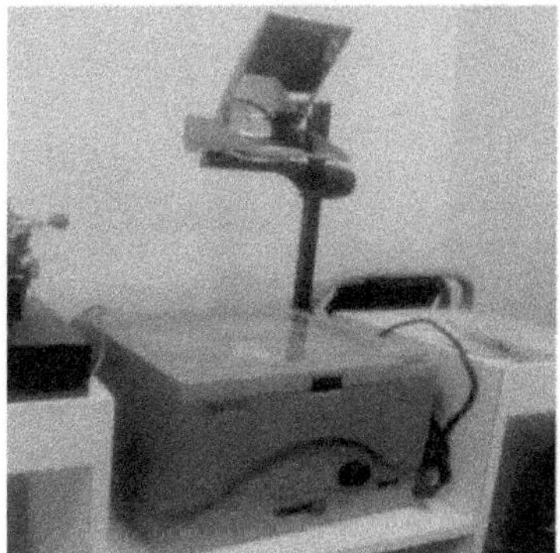

Figure 2.2: Slide projector. Source.

For the development of automotive electrical training, the teaching environments are generally the classroom and the workshop (figure 2.3). In the workshop, the necessary training practices are carried out.

Figure 2.3 : Workshop Pedagogical Environment. Source.

A very common learning object used by teachers in electrical circuit practicals is the didactic model in figure 2.4, for developing electrical circuits. With this resource, students work in teams, developing technical and interpretative skills relating to car electrical circuits.

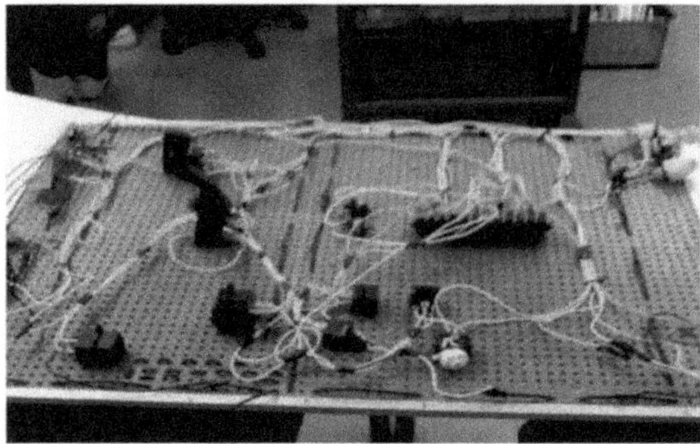
Figura 2.4   - Didactic Electrical Mock-up. Source.

As for consumables for the construction of the electrical circuits in the didactic model, there is a cost of approximately 200 metres of cable, 3 insulating tapes, 300 male and female terminals and electrical components that get damaged over time, such as relays, light bulbs and electric motors.

Educational software can greatly contribute to student learning in electrical courses. Their technical and pedagogical characteristics can help teachers achieve this goal. According to Franco (2006), implicit needs are also called quality in use and should enable users to achieve goals such as effectiveness, productivity, safety and satisfaction in a specified context of use.

2.4 Computer-Mediated Teaching in Car Electrician Maintenance Training.

. The "S" system, through the CNI (National Council of Industry), took the initiative to promote the digital inclusion of vocational education teachers at SENAI schools. Computers were made available to all vocational teachers in Brazil through the Education for the New Industry Programme.

This initiative motivated the teachers, proposing a new teaching resource and reflecting on teaching practice and the use of computers as a means of facilitating lessons (figure 2.5). However, as well as the computer, the teacher needs other resources, such as a data projector for lectures.

Rodrigues et al. (2008) show that the change in the educator's attitude allows them to socialise their work, leaving aside their isolation. In this way, their work comes from the needs of the students in the construction of knowledge, transforming the educator into an advisor of the teaching and learning processes.

Figure 2.5: The computer used by the teacher as a teaching resource. Source.

Teachers have their own teaching methods and many options for using teaching resources, but some teachers who received these computers through the project still use traditional methods.

> Nowadays, the computer has become an artefact that both stores and manipulates information and promotes its dissemination via the Internet. However, its use as a pedagogical tool is not yet fully functional (TAVARES, 2010, p. 5).

The Computer Laboratory (figure 2.6) is an environment for computer-mediated study. This space is often used by teachers without much purpose, but only to access the internet. In automotive electricity classes, this teaching space is not exploited due to the lack of interactive software and teachers linked to technology and educational programmes.

Figure 2.6: The computer lab - teaching environment. Source.

In teachers' didactic activities, it is common to use the computer only as a tool for lectures with the help of the Power Point programme and for researching digitised technical literature.

Many students use computers on a daily basis, accessing social networks via the internet. On student use of computers. Teachers could take advantage of this situation and offer free educational software on the contents of an automotive electrical course. For this to happen, it is necessary to encourage the use of appropriate digital resources for learning. ICT can very well help facilitate student learning.

Learning electrical circuits requires not only the student's interest and concentration, but also the didactic resources available for proper learning. Schools still use conventional resources and methods to teach electrical circuits. According to Franzoni, Laburú and Silva (2010), it is common for conventional diagrams to be introduced at the beginning of the study of electrical circuits. Developing a teaching style in which the teacher passes on the content using traditional pedagogical techniques can produce unmotivated students.

In order for professionals to be able to carry out vehicle electrical maintenance, they need to have a good grasp of the electrical circuit and thus be able to work out the logic of the diagnosis, consulting and interpreting the electrical diagram so that the repair can be carried out. All of this requires the student to have a contemplative capacity, something that many students and professionals in the field still struggle with. During their training, some students even drop out of the course or have no interest in studying other electrical technology because they find the knowledge difficult and tedious to grasp.

Because it requires a certain degree of abstraction, teaching electrical circuits is usually a tedious task for most students, and learning ends up becoming mere memorisation and mechanical operations. Simply memorising mechanical operations in the study of electricity can result in professionals who are unprepared for electrical diagnoses.

The demands of the modern world, due to these difficulties, mean that vocational training schools are becoming increasingly attuned to teaching resources that improve the training of these professionals. Information technology has led to the integration of communication via computer networks in various sectors of society in order to make various human development processes possible. In this respect, the school must bring the resources of the productive environment into the classroom, teaching how to use them responsibly and more professionally.

CHAPTER 3

THE EXPERIENCE OF PREVIOUS *SOFTWARES* - Similar *software*

There are currently many learning objects to help with the process of learning automotive electricity. However, some of them focus on basic and fundamental electrical circuits, but there are no media resources that go into more detail on car-specific circuits, and there are no programmes with a virtual laboratory for making circuits in order to better retain knowledge. Many are tutorial-type programmes with theoretical and conceptual subjects, with animations, but without many specific details on electrical circuits.

3.1 Software used to teach automotive electricity

A lot of educational software can be found on the internet through the educational repositories available to schools and the general community; these can be used in electricity lessons as a teaching tool.

Most of these educational programmes cover basic electrical content, but software specific to automotive electricity is hard to find, especially software that meets the course's expectations in terms of content and regional requirements. Undoubtedly, finding more free software as educational resources would make the teaching and learning process more dynamic and motivating.

> The use of computers allied to blackboards, chalk and textbooks, together with teaching-learning methodologies and teachers, has facilitated the acceleration of the teaching-learning process, providing students with interaction with the content, through animations, visualisations and checks available when using these educational softwares (OLIVEIRA, AMARAL, DOMINGOS, 2011, p. 84).

Many educational software programmes used in the automotive sector are the property of car manufacturers. This means that the use of these programmes is limited only to the automaker's teacher, who often cannot release the resource due to the confidentiality contract for information and teaching resources signed between the automaker and the educational institution providing training services.

In electricity lessons, some teachers try to use educational software. This experience has enabled a new way of working and the students have enjoyed the lessons more. Ferreira (2010) states that by using computer resources in the classroom, schools will be able to create learning spaces in which students research, carry out anticipations and simulations, check out previous ideas and implement them. When learning automotive electricity, this learning space could be significant for the development of students' knowledge.

Below we describe the programmes and the main characteristics of these educational softwares that have some similarity to the proposed programme.

3.1.1 Building and Testing Electrical Circuits Software

This programme belongs to Experiential Physics and can be downloaded from the teacher portal repository (http://portaldoprofessor.mec.gov.br). The software covers basic secondary education and can be applied to automotive electricity. The programme's content covers fundamental electrical circuits, resistor association theory, generators and accumulators (batteries), and electrical instruments. Figure 3.1 shows the main screen of the software with the navigation icons.

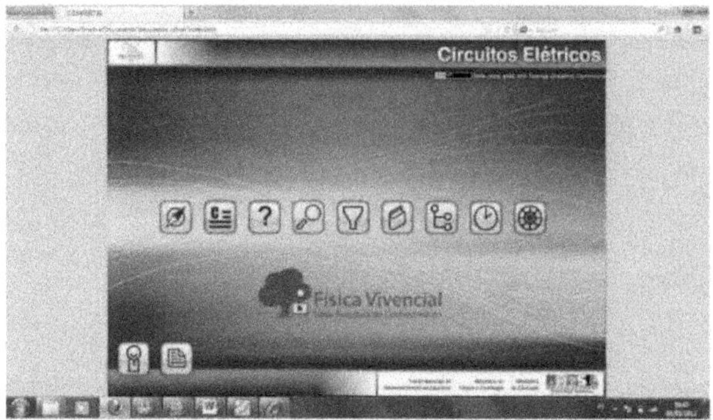

Figure 3.1 - Main screen of the *Software* building and testing electrical circuits, main screen. Source Available: *www.portaldoprofessor.com.br* accessed on 8/05/2012.

The resource has a virtual laboratory for carrying out activities (figure 3.2), enabling simulated experimentation with electrical circuits and electrical measurements with multimeter-type instruments.

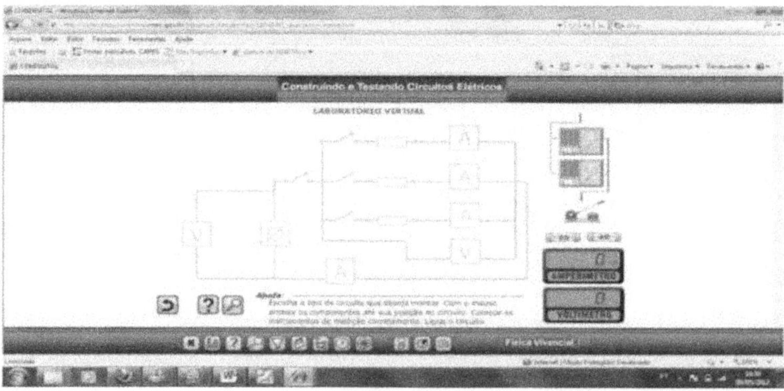

Figure 3.2 - Virtual laboratory building the circuit - Source www.portaldoprofessor.com.br. accessed on 8/05/2012.

The software has video lessons and can be accessed via the "knowledge production" icon. This allows students to ask questions while watching the teacher demonstrate the circuits.

3.1.2 Educational software **CD EL1 V1 CBT**

This educational software is the property of Renault S/A and is used in the professional retraining of the dealership's maintenance network. The aim of the resource is to train its professionals in basic automotive electricity. The teaching resource is an interactive tutorial (figure 3.2) with non-linear navigability. The programme includes animations and audio in line with the proposed content.

The student can carry out the training asynchronously in the workshop or at home, and the teacher can use it as a teaching resource in the lecture method. The programme contains information specific to cars, such as the charging and starting system, lighting and signalling.

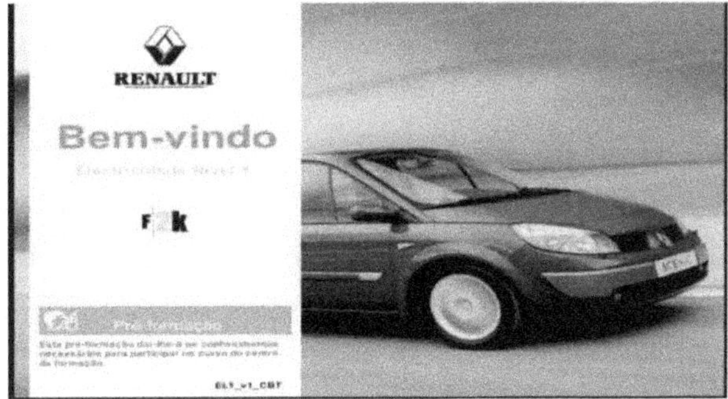

Figure 3.3: Initial screen of the training software. Source: Renault training programme.

The software has a variety of features, with a user-friendly interface that is not complex to access, in other words, it is very intuitive. There are animations of electrical circuits, but there is no virtual laboratory for building electrical circuits. Figure 3.4 shows the programme's index, where students can access each lesson and watch the content explained.

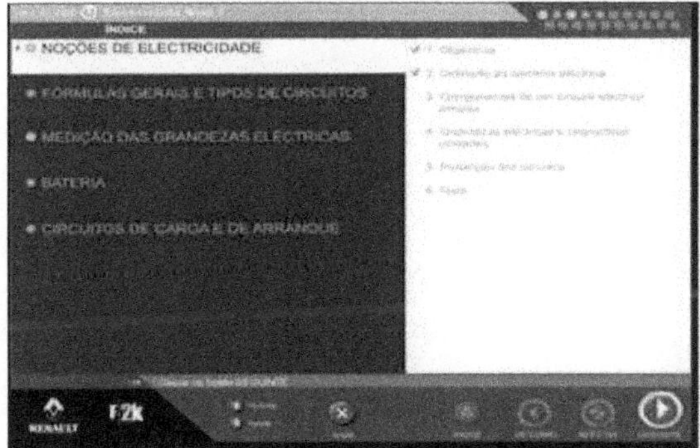

Figure 3.4: Activity Index. Source: Renault training programme.

The programme is in Portuguese and requires a password to access, as the resource is the property of the car manufacturer.

3.1.3 MWM Basic Electricity Programme

MWM[3] is a major automotive company whose best-selling product is diesel engines. This company also

---

[3] MWM Motores Diesel Ltda. (MWM), originally named Motoren Werke Mannheim AG, is a Brazilian company that

has a partnership with SENAI, which trains professionals in the heavy vehicle maintenance network.

The software developed by MWM uses an interactive tutorial-type teaching resource with non-linear navigability (figure 3.5). The programme has few animations and no audio. The programme is intended for use in electrical training. The software is the exclusive property of MWM and is only used as a teaching resource for teachers approved by the car manufacturer.

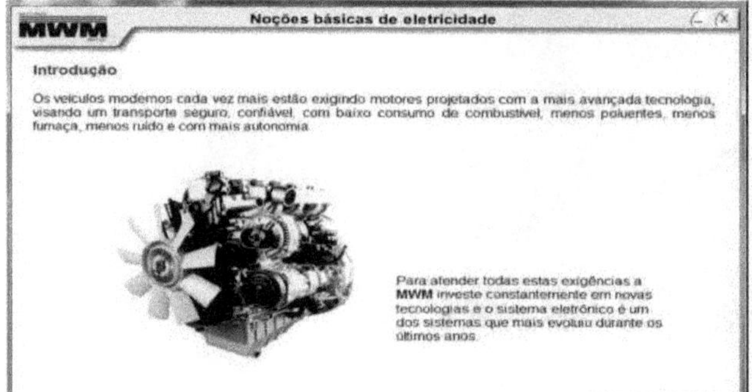

Figure 3.5: Introduction to the resource. Source: MWM training programme.

The programme develops the content of basic electricity, focusing on fundamental electrical circuits, the association of resistors and OHM's Law (figure 3.6). For the motor manufacturer, it is important to emphasise the basic aspects of electricity, in order to recognise this deficiency in its maintenance network professionals.

Figure 3.6: Association of resistors in series. Source: MWM training programme.

The software does not have a virtual laboratory for building electrical circuits, so it is limited to fundamental electrical circuits.

3.1.4 Faraday's Electromagnetic Lab Educational *Software*

---

produces diesel combustion engines for vehicles. It was founded in 1922, bought by Klöckner-Humboldt-Deutz AG (KHD) in 1985 and sold to Navistar International in March 2005.

This *software* can be *downloaded* from the teacher's portal (www.portaldoprofessor.com.br). The *software* makes it possible to develop simulations of magnetism (figure 3.7) and electromagnetism without a laboratory set up to carry out these experiments.

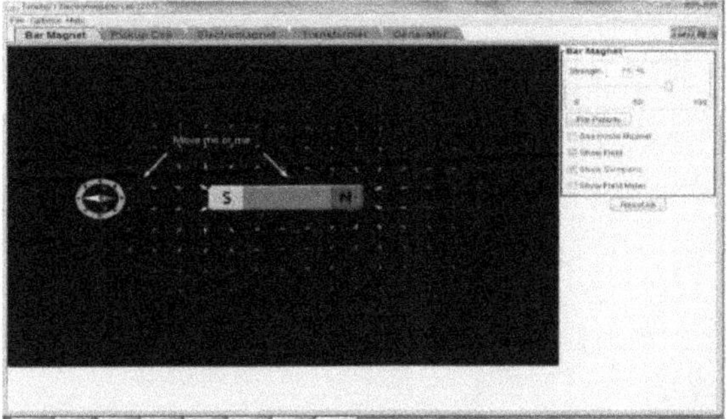

Figure 3.7: Faraday's software simulating magnetism. Source:
www.portaldoprofessor.com.br access : 12/03/2013

. Figure 3.8 shows a screen from the programme in which the student simulates a charging circuit, using the tap to activate the water. The software has been programmed in the Java language[4] , and the resource is very easy for students to use. The difficulty is that the menu is in English, which may be a problem for some users.

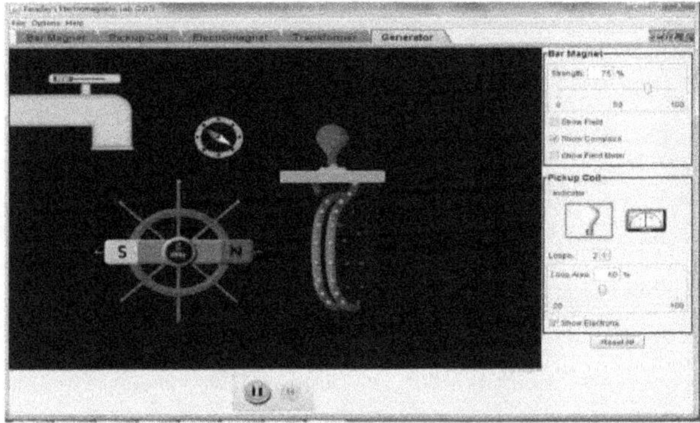

Figure 3.8: Load system simulation. Source: www.portaldoprofessor.com.br access: 14/03/2013.

3.1.5 **Edison** software from designsoft

The Edison software has several versions available on the internet. The programme is proprietary software and can be downloaded by purchasing it from the website (http://www.edisonlab.com/English/edison).

The software is a simulator of electrical and electronic circuits. There is a virtual laboratory in which the user interacts with the electrical components available, making basic and complex electrical circuits. Figure 3.9 shows the virtual laboratory for developing electrical circuits by selecting the components you want to

---

[4]Java is an object-orientated programming language developed in the 1990s by a team of programmers led by James Gosling at Sun Microsystems.

connect.

Figure 3.9: Virtual laboratory. Source: http://www.edisonlab.com/English/edison Accessed on 25/03/2013.

In the "Edison" *software*, the electrical components are presented in real format, which makes the cognitive load very light for understanding the circuit at the time of construction. As the student builds the circuit, the programme executes the electrical diagram. Figure 3.10 shows the assembled schematic on the left and the wiring diagram on the right.

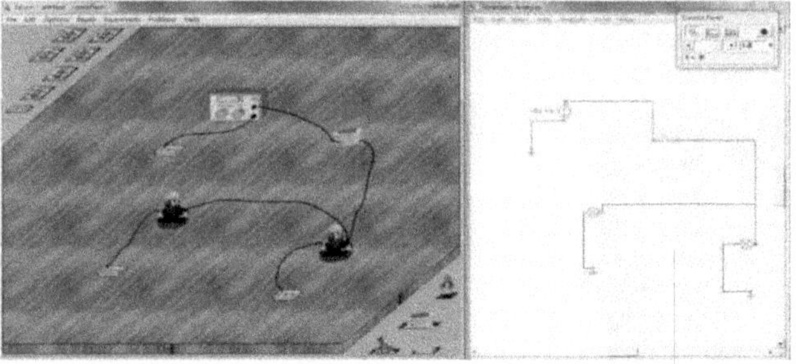

Figure 3.10:   Parallel circuit with components. Source: http://www.edisonlab.com/English/edison Accessed: 25/03/2013.

Teachers can use this software in automotive electricity lessons, as the virtual laboratory gives students the opportunity to build various circuits.

With the electrical circuits developed, students will be able to virtually measure voltage, resistance and current values using the educational software. This practice of simulating electrical circuits is very useful for students.

CHAPTER 4

METHODOLOGICAL PROCEDURES FOR BUILDING THE ELECTROAUTOS SOFTWARE

All educational software development involves professionals in the fields of computer science, programming, graphic design, pedagogy and teaching, with the aim of achieving programme quality and acceptance by the target audience. For this to be a reality, there is a need to adopt a methodology to standardise software development procedures.

Methodologies have a sequence of phases in order to enable continuous flows of corrections. Based on the methodology, product development can begin with good communication between the professionals involved, capable of satisfactorily achieving the desired requirements.

Various methodologies have been published in the literature for creating learning objects. Some examples are Vaughan (2010), Costa (1998), Johnson (1992), Oliveira, Bassani and others.

Table 4.1 below shows the characteristics and processes of each author cited and the difference between each methodology.

Stages	Vaughan	Johnson	Costa	Oliveira	Bassani	Sophia	
1	Idea definition	Definition	Design	Choice of content	Requirements survey	Process ess project	proc
2	Planning	Development ento	Realisation	Analysis	Analysis	Process ess development	proc
3	Production	Evaluation and maintenance	T est and validation	Concept map	Project/prototyp ing	Process ess distribution	proc
4	Evaluation		Diffusion	Navigational architecture	This e validation		
5	Distribution		Exploitation	Storyboar d			
6				Implementat ion			
7				Documentati on of use			
8				Utilisation evaluation and maintenanc e			

Table 4.1: Stages of the methodology according to different authors. Source: Article - An experience for defining a **storyboard** in a collaborative development methodology for learning objects.

There are also environments for creating educational software, developed by universities and creative organisations. These include the Virtual Interactive Education Network (RIVED), run by the Ministry of Education (MEC), and the Production of Interactive Environments and Learning Objects, run by the Federal University of Ceará (PROATIVA).

The SOPHIA Project comprises a repository of learning objects designed to support students in carrying out activities and with content to support the subjects of the Technology in Systems Analysis and Development (TADS) course at the Vale do Itajaí University in Santa Catarina. The course is in the

The aim is to train professionals in the field of Computing and Informatics to work in the development, implementation and management of information systems.

The Sophia project comprises a repository of learning objects designed to support students in carrying out activities and with content to support the subjects.

3.2 The Choice of Methodology

For the development of the ELETROAUTOS software, the SOPHIA methodology was chosen, which comprises three important stages (Table 4.2), from the design to the implementation of the programme.

Step 1	1. DESIGN PROCESS
Stage 2	2. DEVELOPMENT PROCESS
Step 3	3. DISTRIBUTION PROCESS

Table 4.2: Sophia sub-process.

In building the ELETROAUTOS software, the three stages were followed with activities defined and organised by the development team (coordinator, teacher, designer, programmer). The team will have defined responsibilities with the following functions.

1 Coordinator: responsible for managing activities and communication between team members.

2 Content teacher: responsible for the pedagogical part, content and evaluation of the product.

3 Designer: responsible for developing animated content, colours and videos in the programme.

4 Programmer: implement the programme in a specific machine language to generate the contents in the software.

4.2 Project Process

In the first phase of the programme construction process, the following artefacts were developed:

- Artefact I - the teaching plan.

- Artefact II - development plan.

- Artefact III - software structure.

22

- Artefact I: Pedagogical Plan

The purpose of the ELETROAUTOS software is to be a tutorial-type resource, with exercises from reinforcement and interactive with the virtual laboratory, in the pedagogical methodology of vocational education. The software's target audience was students starting vocational training in automotive electricity, according to the training itinerary.

The aim of building the software was to have a specific teaching tool for automotive electricity in automotive electrical circuits.

The following table contains the educational characteristics of the ELETROAUTOS programme.

Items	Features	Pedagogical aspects
1	Virtual practices	Developing electrical circuits on the computer.
2	Safe practices	Development of activities with the teacher's guidance, using the computer before the practicals in the vehicle.
3	Dynamic lessons	Using the computer as an interactive and motivating medium.
4	Sensitisation	Use of ICTs, preparing students for contact with computers in the labour market.
5	Resource of medium interactivity	0 programme has an index in which the student can interact, using the programme's logical commands.
6	Learning and simulating	0 *software* has electrical circuits as a learning resource; the user develops the content and then simulates and builds the same automotive electrical circuit.
7	Autonomy	0 ELETROAUTOS software is intuitive and the user is encouraged to discover the correct way to assemble electrical circuits. To do this, they must first study the circuit so that they can then carry out the assembly.

Box 4.3: Pedagogical aspects of the **software.**

A roadmap (table below) was developed by the pedagogical team for the duties and actions of each team member in the process of developing the ELETROAUTOS programme.

Responsible	Actions
Teachers/coordinator	Definition of discipline and way of working in automotive maintenance teaching activities.
Coordinator	1. Target audience research.
	2. Survey of educational requirements. 3. Pedagogical planning of courses. 4. Co-ordination of the other teams.
Teachers content	1 Elaboration or reuse of teaching situations and content. 2. Content research. 3. Mapping the content to be covered. 4. Specification of additional content. 5. Content evaluation at the production stage.

Box 4.4: Responsible parties and actions.

Artefact II: Development plan

A timetable was also developed for the realisation of the project, defining responsibilities and dates with the important actions for the progress of the work. With this action plan, the coordinator was responsible for monitoring the activities.

Date	Actions	Responsible
Dec/2010	- Definition of the subject and way of working in automotive maintenance teaching activities and target audience.	Teacher / coordinator.

January February	- Survey of programme requirements and the pedagogical plan.	Coordinator.
March / 2011		
April May June July Z2012	• Content search. Specification of additional content. • Content evaluation at the production stage.	Content teacher.
August a December / 2012	- Development of content in the form of media, implementation of teaching situations.	Des/gner/programmer.
January a August / 2013	- Access the programme and take the assessment.	Students and teachers.

Table 4.5: Action timetable.

- Artefact III: Structure of the ELETROAUTOS *software*

The ELETROAUTOS *software* comes with a *Flash* programming language, with the aim of creating options for students' virtual and autonomous activities, proposing theoretical content, simulating automotive electrical circuits and providing a virtual environment for exercises.

The choice of programme in which to run the *software* was a decision made by the development team. For the ELETROAUTOS software, it was necessary to think about a programming language that would be easy to use in order to achieve the objectives. Choosing a programming language that has interactive features, producing images and simulations, is fundamental. In the team's view, the *Flash* language fulfils these expectations.

The Adobe Flash programme known as Flash Professional MX flash 8.0 is an authoring language used to build interactive animations and digital content. Muerer, Steffani (2009) comment that *flash* provides tools that allow you to import figures and animations whose primitive characteristics, such as colour, size, movements and shapes, can be modified.

The Flash MX programme can be associated with other languages due to its flexibility and low level of complexity. The characteristics of the Flash MX programme are considered complicit in the development of many learning objects, due to its flexibility and lower level of complexity compared to other programmes such as JAVA and PHP. Its flexibility gives it the power to display digitised content in a totally accessible way.

• Didactic content of the programme

The content of the software was defined by the pedagogical team (teachers and coordinator). It contains eight electrical circuits: three fundamental electrical circuits and five car-specific circuits from the Lighting and Signalling subject.

The description of the fundamental circuits is defined below with function and characteristics,

24

according to Irwin (2005, p. 32).

<u>Fundamental circuits</u>

"A circuit is a set of interconnected electronic components."

• Simple electrical circuit - this will be an element interconnected by conductive wires fed by an energy accumulator.

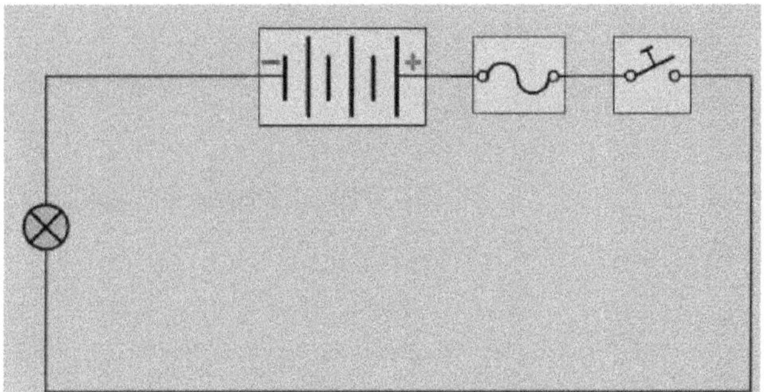

Figure 4.1 - Simple circuit.

• Series electrical circuit - a circuit formed by a single loop and connected by two or more elements in series when they are passed through by the same current.

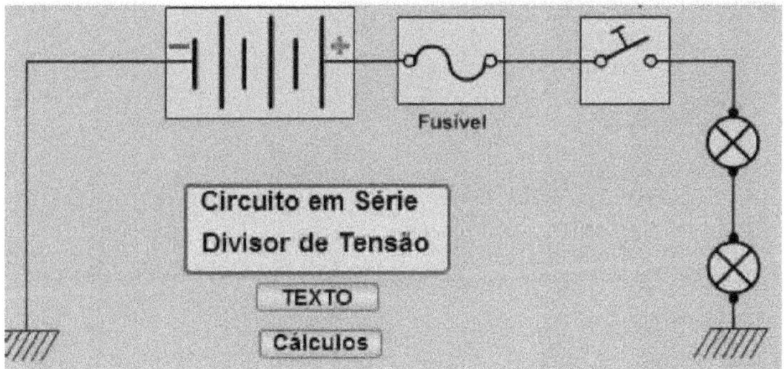

Figure 4.2 - Series circuit.

• Parallel electrical circuit - formed by a single pair of nodes in which two or more elements are connected in parallel when they are subjected to the same voltage.

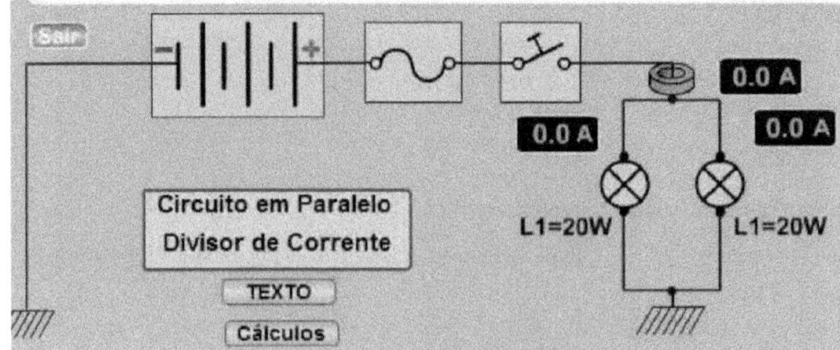

Figure 4.3 - Parallel circuit.

<u>- The specific circuits of the Lighting and Signalling discipline</u>

The respective contents are defined and based on the CNI-SENAI vehicle electronics material (2010):

- Ground connection (figure 4.4) - an electrical circuit always ends with a return to the source. Manufacturers often use the chassis or bodywork as a return conductor. These metal conductors are called ground.

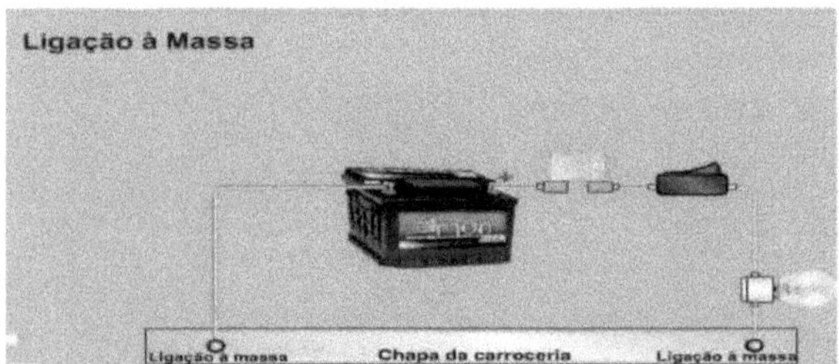

Figura 4.4   mass connection

- Reverse circuit (figure 4.5) - the white reverse lights switch on automatically when reverse gear is engaged to illuminate the rear of the vehicle.

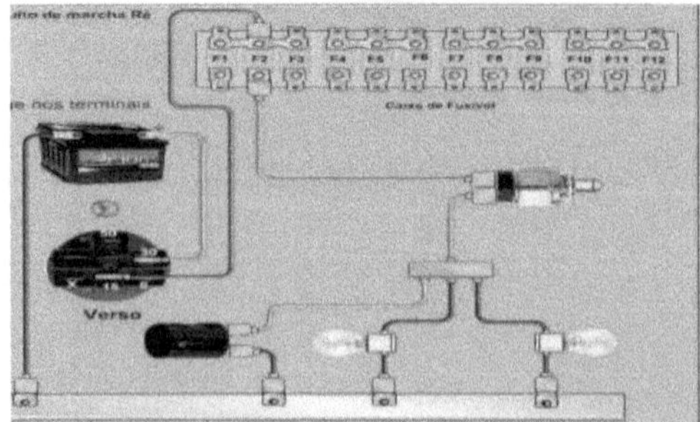

Figura 4.5   - Reverse circuit

- Brake circuit (figure 4.6) - the brake lights play an important role with regard to driving

26

safety. It is controlled by a switch fixed to the footplate at the end of the brake pedal.

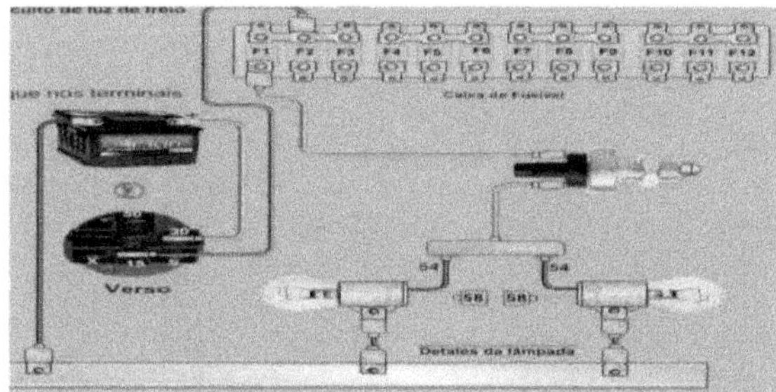

Figura 4.6   - Brake light circuit

- Parking light (figure 4.7) - the parking light allows the driver to see if there is another vehicle.

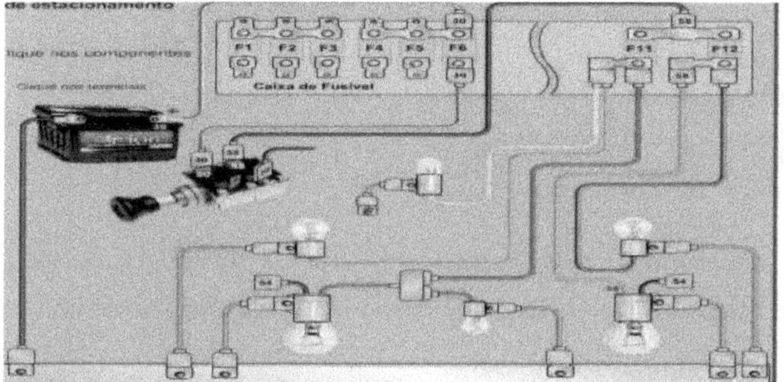

Figura 4.7   - Parking light circuit

- Headlight circuit (figure 4.8) - the proper functioning of headlights is essential for the safety of drivers, as it allows them to benefit from good visibility on the road during night-time driving.

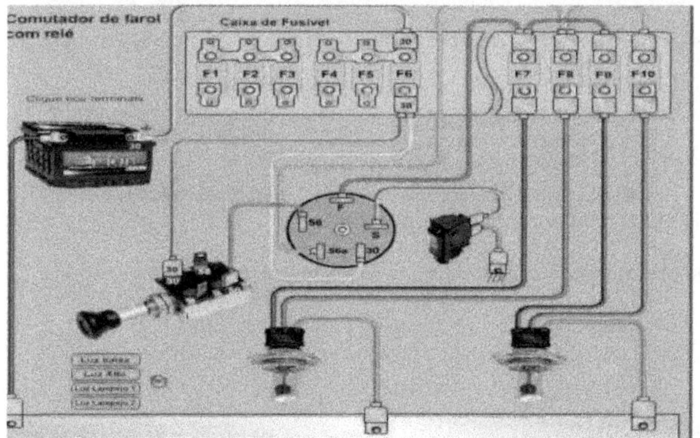

Figure 4.8 - Headlight circuit

- User and software relationship

The use case diagram used by the development team in the graphic below shows how the user's

27

relationship with the ELETROAUTOS educational software was defined when carrying out the learning activities.

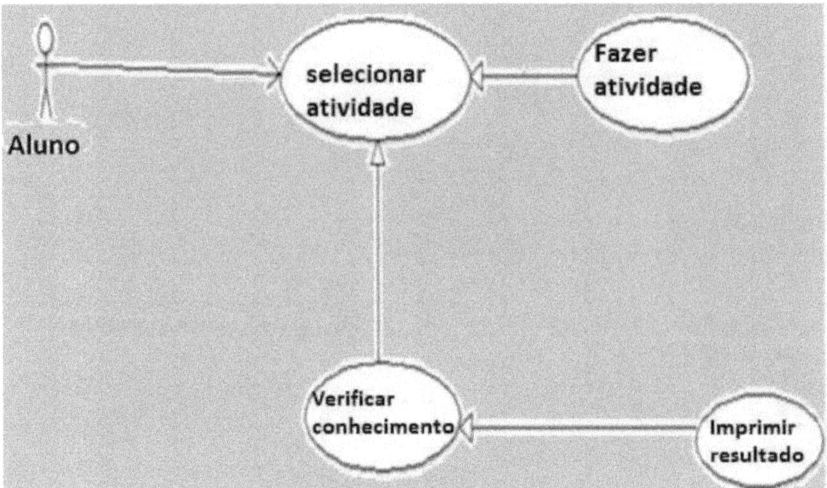

Diagram 4.1: ELETROAUTOS **software** use case. Source: ArgoUML.

. According to diagram 4.1, the student selects the activity, studies the electrical circuit and then does the fixation activity at the end of all the activities; he checks what he has learnt through a final assessment.

Ratio: table of contents and contents

With regard to the proposed content, there was a relationship between the circuits and the virtual laboratory. All the circuits had a relationship with the index and the circuit with the virtual laboratory for the construction of the circuit developed.

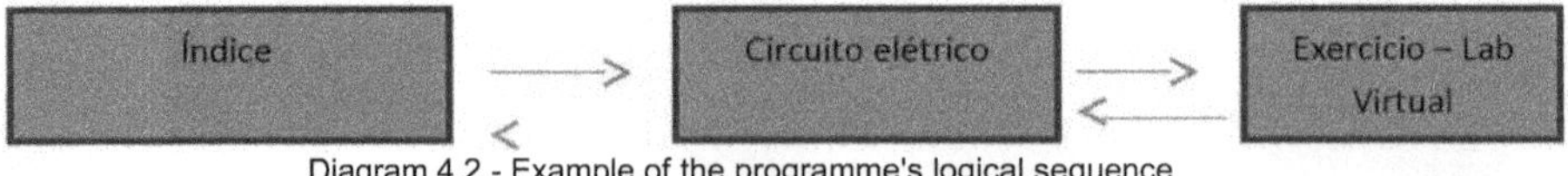

Diagram 4.2 - Example of the programme's logical sequence

These screens show an example of the programme's logical sequence in relation to the circuits seen in diagram 4.2.

4.3   Project Development Process

For the development team, the dynamic with the cover image (Figure 4.3) arouses the curiosity of the student to access the software. The table of contents shows lighting circuits, which is the content of the programme's electrical circuits.

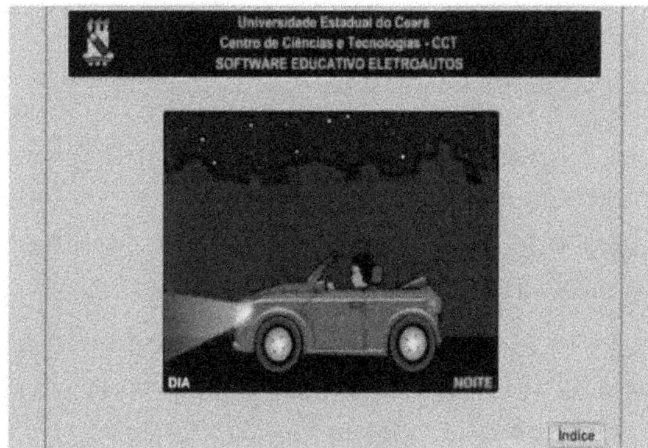

Figure 4.9: Definition of the **software** cover.

The table of contents (Figure 4.10) contains the list of circuits arranged in rectangular icons with the name of each circuit you want to study. The icons direct the student to the content, providing access to each circuit.

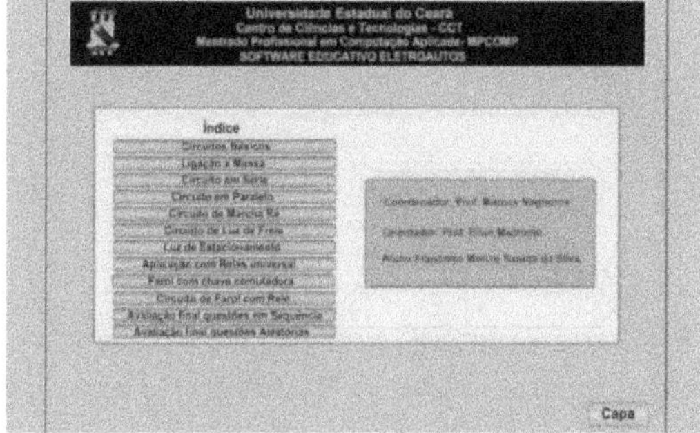

Figure 4.10: Index with circuit icons.

The layout of the screen shows a pleasant aesthetic with colours that are not too strong. In the corner of the screen, there is an icon with the name CAPA, intuitively directing the student back to the previous screen.

Figure 4.11 shows the simple basic circuit screen, in case the student wants to return to the INDEX. They can click on the icon in the corner of the screen.

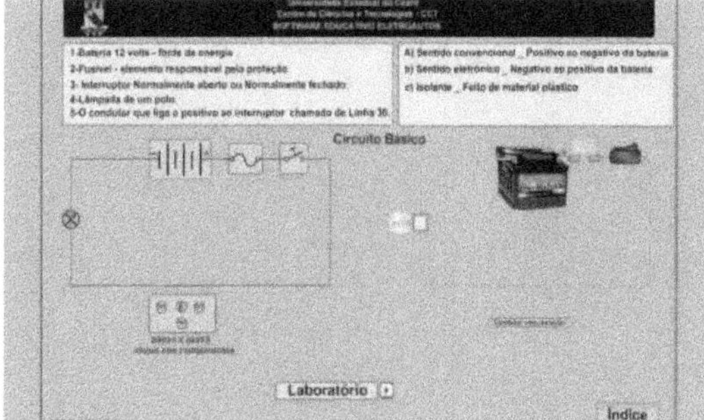

Figure 4.11: Basic ELECTROAUTOS circuit.

When the student is analysing the circuit, they can click on the electrical components (switches, battery, light bulb) in the diagram, and there will be an animation of the electrons passing through the conductive wire from the positive pole to the negative pole of the battery, showing the student the behaviour of the electrons as they drive the light bulb. This animation is important because it shows that the conventional direction of the electric current is opposite to the direction of the flow of electrons.

The programme contains information on the components involved in the electrical circuit. As the student interacts with the circuit, they click on the STEP BY STEP icon on the left-hand side of the screen, and the circuit is formed in the pattern of an electrical diagram with the shape of the real components.

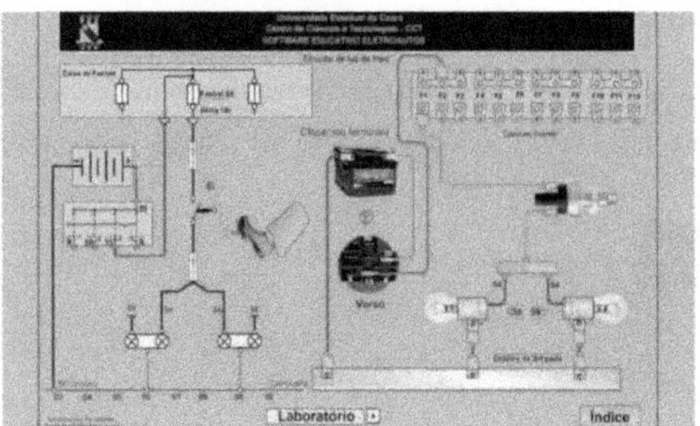

Figure 4.12 - Study environment - brake light circuit.

In the brake light circuit (Figure 4.12), there are two examples of different circuit formats: one represents the electrical diagram format; the other the circuit format with the actual components. The picture, which shows the driver's foot on the pedal, helps the student to understand how this electrical circuit is activated. The virtual laboratory (Figure 4.13) is designed for experimental assembly of electrical circuits, without the need to spend on electrical consumables or break any electrical components in the learning process.

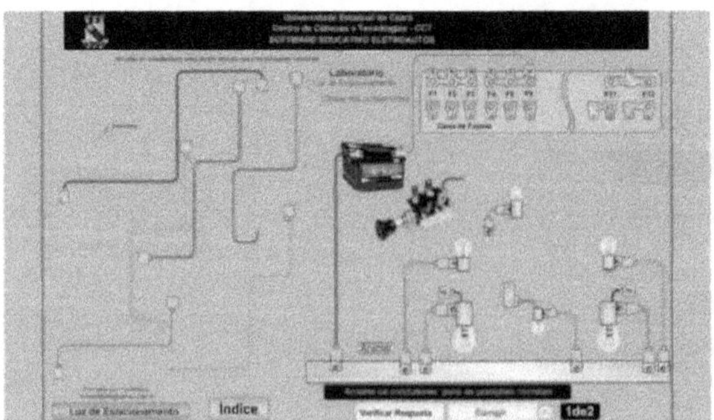

Figure 4.13: The virtual laboratory of the parking light circuit.

The virtual laboratory will always finalise the learning of each circuit with an electrical circuit construction activity, showing the result of the circuits assembled with a correct or incorrect answer. This allows students to test whether they have actually learnt how to make the circuit themselves.

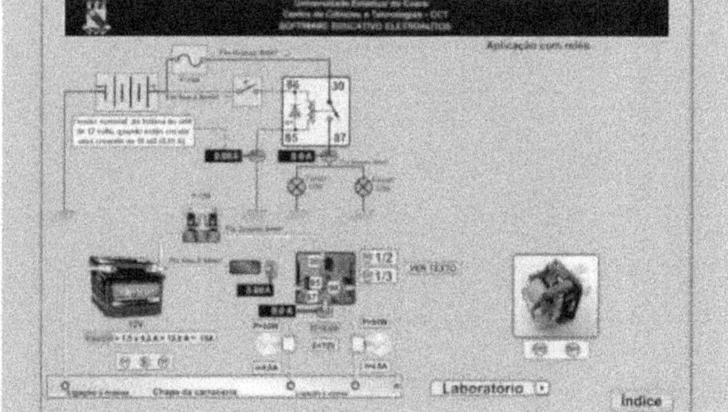
Figure 4.14: Diagram of the universal relay.

Another aspect that the software offers for student learning is up-to-date technological information using more complex components in the car. The diagram in figure 4.14 shows a circuit with a universal relay and its application in an electrical circuit.

4.4   Distribution and initial tests

The programme was distributed to the automotive electrical apprenticeship and vocational training classes, when the product was presented to the students in order to test the programme.

The didactic method used with the resource was organised in such a way that the students worked in pairs with a computer, in order to check how well they were integrating it through the construction of the proposed circuits and in the exercises, observing whether any errors in the programme needed to be corrected.

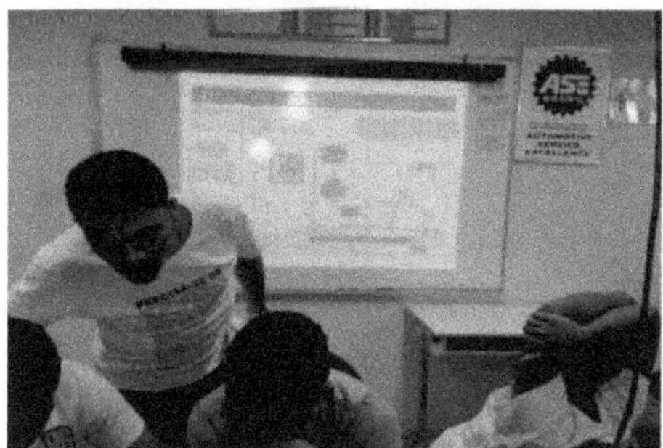
Figure 4.15: PRONATEC students. Own source.

After distributing the ELETROAUTOS programme, a 20-question Likert Scale questionnaire was carried out (Appendix A) based on Nokelaine's (2006) pedagogical usability. In this way, the students gave feedback on the programme, checking for positive and negative aspects.

The questionnaire applied to a class is based on ten pedagogical usability fundamentals, listed in table 4.4 below. When applying the questionnaire, the meaning of each criterion was shown in order to check whether the programme had pedagogical attributes in its ease of use.

Quantity	Criteria	Questions	
2	Student control	1	2
2	Student activity	3	4
2	Co-operative and collaborative learning and motivation	5	6
2	Object orientation	7	8
2	Applicability	9	10
2	Added value	11	12
2	Motivation	13	14
2	Evaluation of prior knowledge	15	16
2	Flexibility	17	18
2	Feedback	19	20

Table 4.6: Questions / distributed questions - Own source.

Table 4.7 shows the tabulated results of the questionnaire worked on with 20 students who took part in the distribution of ELETROAUTOS.

Item	1	2	3	4	5	6	7	8	9	10	11	12	13	14	15	16	17	18	19	20	21	22	Average
1	4	5	4	4	4	4	4	5	4	4	4	4	5	4	4	5	5	5	5	5	4	5	4.40
2	4	5	5	5	5	4	5	5	5	5	5	5	5	5	4	5	5	5	5	5	5	4	4.81
3	2	4	3	4	2	4	4	2	3	5	4	3	4	2	5	4	4	5	4	5	2	4	3,45
4	4	5	4	5	5	5	5	4	4	5	4	5	5	5	5	5	4	5	4	5	5	4	4.63
5	4	5	4	5	3	5	4	1	4	4	4	4	5	5	4	5	5	5	5	4	5	4	4.27
6	4	5	4	5	5	5	5	5	4	5	5	5	5	5	3	4	5	1	4	5	5	5	4.50
7	4	4	5	4	4	5	4	3	4	5	4	4	5	5	5	5	5	5	4	5	5	4	4.45
8	3	5	5	4	5	5	5	5	4	4	4	5	5	4	5	4	5	5	5	5	4	4	4.54
9	5	4	4	4	5	5	5	4	4	5	5	4	5	5	5	4	5	5	4	5	5	4	4.59
10	4	2	4	4	5	4	4	1	5	1	4	4	5	5	5	4	1	1	5	5	4	4	3.68
11	4	5	5	5	5	5	4	4	5	5	4	3	5	5	5	5	5	5	5	5	5	4	4.68
12	5	4	4	4	4	4	4	4	3	4	4	5	5	5	5	5	4	5	5	4	5	4	4.36
13	5	5	5	5	5	4	5	4	4	5	5	5	5	5	5	5	5	5	5	5	5	4	4.81
14	4	5	4	4	4	5	5	4	4	4	5	4	5	5	5	4	4	5	5	5	4	4	4.45
15	4	4	4	2	4	4	4	5	4	4	5	5	4	5	5	3	1	2	5	4	5	4	3.95
16	4	5	4	2	4	3	4	5	5	3	4	4	5	5	4	4	2	2	4	5	5	4	3.95
17	4	5	4	4	5	5	4	3	5	5	5	5	5	5	4	4	5	5	5	5	4	4	4.54
18	4	4	4	4	5	5	5	4	4	4	5	3	5	5	5	4	5	5	5	5	4	4	4.45
19	4	4	4	2	4	4	1	4	4	2	5	4	5	5	3	3	5	5	4	5	4	4	3.86
20	4	4	4	4	4	4	5	3	4	5	5	4	5	5	4	4	5	5	4	3	5	4	4.27

Table 4.7: Survey results.

With the data tabulated in Table 4.7, the average for each criterion was calculated by dividing the sum by the number of students. Each criterion in the questionnaire is identified by two questions on the survey form. Therefore, when defining the average for each criterion, the questions were added together and divided by two to obtain the final average (Table 4.8).

item	Questions	Average
1	Student control	4.60
2	Student activity	4.04
3	Co-operative and collaborative learning and motivation	4.38
4	Object orientation	4.49
5	Applicability	4.13

6	Added value	4.52
7	Motivation	4.63
8	Evaluation of previous knowledge	3.95
9	Flexibility	4.49
10	*Feedback*	4.06

Table 4.8: Evaluation criteria and averages.

Graph 4.1 shows the Pareto diagram where the results are presented.

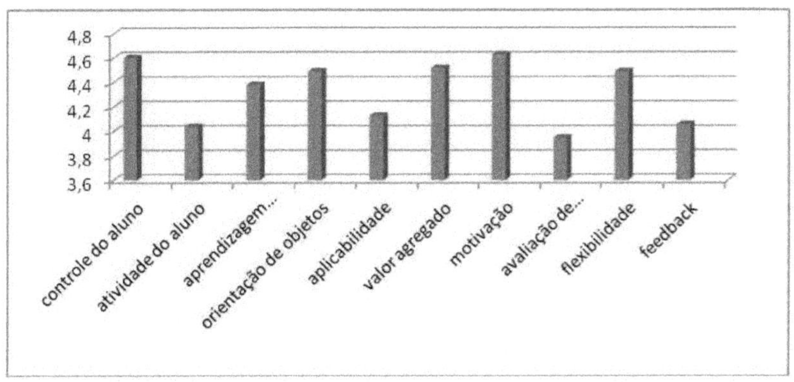

Graph 4.1: Criteria assessed for pedagogical usability.

4.4.1 Initial conclusions

An initial evaluation of the programme by the students showed that the motivational aspects generated by the programme were the most outstanding point, achieving the highest score.

Some opinions and suggestions for improving the software were also noted through the teachers' observations. Below is a table of the strengths and weaknesses highlighted at the time of application.

STRENGTHS	POINTS TO CHANGE
Images and illustrations.	Other types of car circuits.
Illustrations of the material and easy language.	They get stuck in some electrical circuits in the exercises.
Dynamic interface and good usability.	You can't change any of the content or images.
Content on subjects specific to car electrics.	Requires knowledge of flash to improve the programme.
Virtual fixation activity.	Very strong colours.
Didactic resource to help with lessons.	Portuguese mistakes.
Good portability and graininess.	

Table 4.9: Strengths and weaknesses.

Some modifications were made to the programme, such as correcting some Portuguese errors and circuits that crashed while the activities were being carried out. Changes were also made to the images and colours of certain animations and other weak points highlighted in the initial research.

CHAPTER 5

TESTING AND VALIDATION OF ELECTROAUTOS SOFTWARE - RESULTS CONCLUSIONS

In order to validate the ELETROAUTOS software for learning car electrical circuits in SENAI classroom courses, two stages of the research were carried out. In the first, a sample of 20 students from the two classes of the automotive electrician mechanic course was used, in the lighting and signalling subject of PRONATEC, which lasts 200 hours. The second stage involved research with 11 students from the Volkswagen dealership's automotive maintenance apprenticeship class, in the lighting and signalling subject.

To check the programme's efficiency, a knowledge assessment was carried out, based on electricity content and electrical diagram interpretation (Appendix B).

When applying the evaluation (Appendix D) to the classes, the PRONATEC class was called class "A", the one in which the educational *software* was applied; the other class was called class "B", in which the traditional method for teaching electrical circuits was used. The aim of the evaluation is to check the performance of the two classes and then carry out a learning analysis of automotive electrical circuits, to find out the results of the classes and whether there has been satisfactory learning progress in the class in which the programme was applied.

5.1 PRONATEC class evaluation

The first aspect of the evaluation was to check whether the ELETROAUTOS *software* had achieved what was expected with regard to the proposed theoretical knowledge of fundamental and specific electrical circuits. To do this, evaluations were set up with subjective questions on certain important electrical issues.

The first question was to identify the main electrical components using a simple circuit (Figure 5.1).

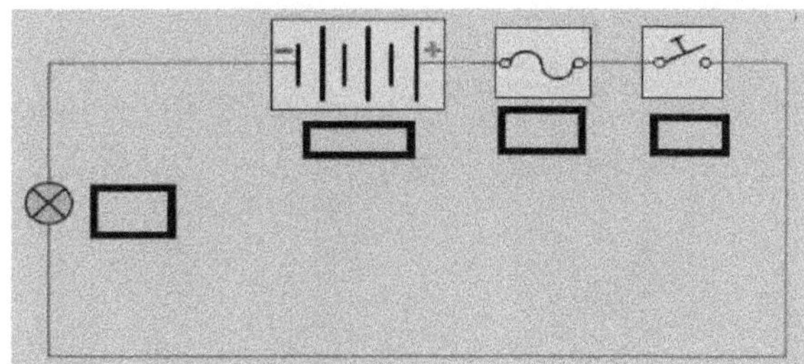

Figure 5.1: Simple circuit.

The aim of this type of question is to see whether the student has learnt to associate the symbology with certain parts when interpreting the electrical diagram. The result was as follows:

List of class "A" and "B".

Classes	Percentage (hits)
A	100
B	60

The second question asked whether the students could identify two basic electrical circuits using the diagrams. The result was this:

Class "A" and Class "B" ratio

Classes	Percentage (hits)
A	100
B	40

The third question asked about the significance of the connection to the mass.

In class "A", all the students defined it correctly. Below are some of the students' definitions:

"A connection made in the body of the vehicle, where it is charged by the negative of the battery" (Marcos).

"Connection to ground, negative battery terminal to connect to the body."
(Afonso).

"The ground connection is the negative of the battery that connects to the vehicle body."
(Wallace)

In class "B", none of the students managed to give a satisfactory answer to such a simple and basic definition of a car's electrical circuit. This question, in the assessment of most of the students, was left blank. Some of the students' definitions were wrong:

"I understand that the mass connection comes from the car itself" (Lucas)

"the entire carcass of the vehicle" (Paul)

"which is the vehicle ground that comes directly from the battery" (Filemon)

In the fourth question, an electrical diagram of a car circuit was shown (Figure 5.2) and the name of the electrical circuit was asked.

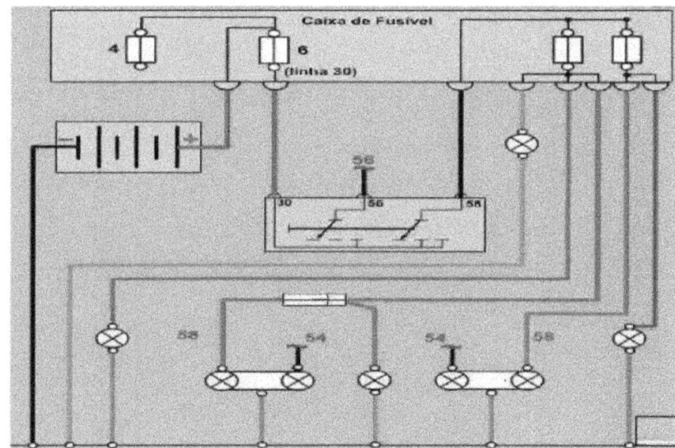

Figure 5.2: Electrical diagram of the parking light system.

The students in class "A" answered 100 per cent correctly, while class "B" didn't give any correct answers.

Another question presented the figure (5.3) of a two-pole headlight bulb (figure 5.3) for the students to define what it represented.

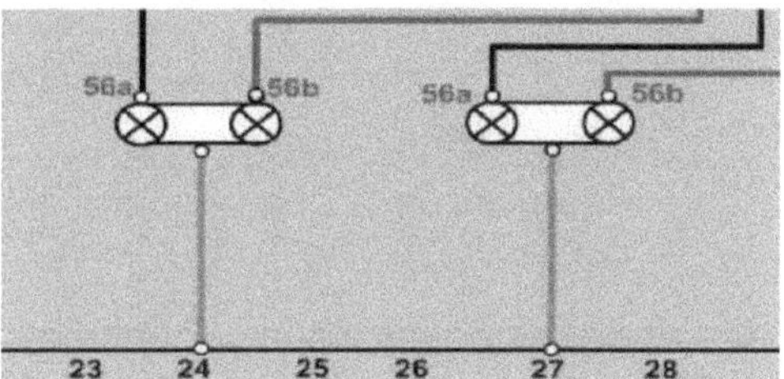

Figure 5.3: Two-pole lamp.

In class "A", everyone gave a satisfactory answer; in class B, only one student answered correctly.

To finalise the assessment, we checked whether the students in classes "A" and "B" knew how to interpret an electrical diagram specific to automotive electricity.

Correctly reading the electrical diagram is an important objective for students to achieve. Class "A", as *jS* recorded, used the *software* to learn electrical circuits.

In the assessment, they were shown the diagram of an electrical circuit, in figure 5.4, for the high and low beam headlights of a Volkswagen Gol car. Ten direct questions were highlighted, and the students had to consult the electrical diagram and answer them. This way, depending on the answer, you can tell whether the students understand the diagram or not.

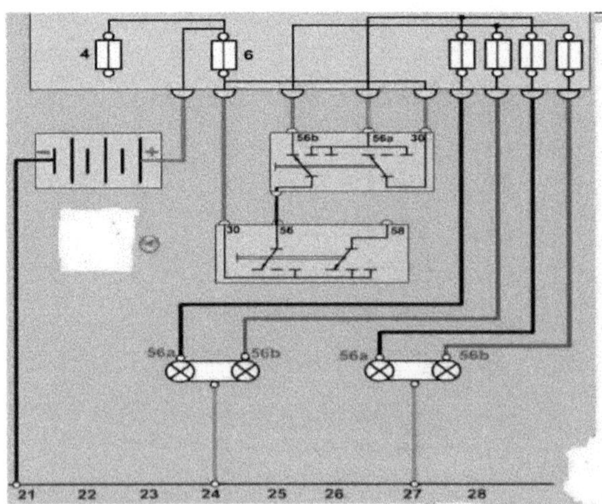

Figure 5.4: Electrical diagram.

The question was asked about the name of the highlighted electrical circuit.

The result, in percentages, was this:

* Class "A"   100 correct
* Class "B"   30 correct

Another question was about the meaning of the figures in the diagram that represent electrical components in symbolic form.

The result, in percentages, was as follows:

* Class "A"   80 correct
* Class "B"   No-one got it right

Another question was about the meaning of the protective fuses and the type of power supply involved in the diagram.

Result, in per cent:

* Class "A"   80 correct
* Class "B"   40 correct

5.2 Evaluation of the Software in the Learning Class

In the apprenticeship class, the subject Electrical Systems for Automotive Lighting and Signalling was developed, with 80 hours of work. At first, the teacher didn't use the software; then the assessment was carried out.

At another point, the software was presented and applied to the leptops to carry out the virtual activities offered by the programme, when possible doubts could be dealt with using the resource. After had finalised the activities, the same assessment was carried out (Appendix "D") to see if there had been any progress in relation to the previous assessment.

Below are some of the evaluation results from the survey:

Question 01 - Knowledge of the main electrical circuit symbols

<u>Without using the *software*</u>

With regard to the symbologies of the components of electrical circuits, the students responded satisfactorily, without the need for any other didactic resource. Only two of them didn't recognise the ground connection symbols.

<u>Using the *software*</u>

After using the programme, 100 per cent of the questions representing automotive electrical components were correct. The two students who didn't recognise the ground connection now answered correctly.

Question 2 - Knowledge of fundamental circuits

<u>Without using the *software*</u>

Two different types of electrical circuits were highlighted in the assessment, one in series and the other in parallel, so that the students could point out the type of circuit in focus. The result was this: only one student didn't recognise the basic electrical circuit. This result is considered very good.

<u>Using the *software*</u>

There was 100 per cent correct identification of the fundamental circuits. The student who left the answer blank in the first assessment corrected it with the correct answer in the second.

Question 3 - Some open-ended topics on electrical circuits were covered to see if the students know how to write about certain topics in vehicle electricity. The results are shown below.

<u>Without using the *software*</u>

- Almost 100 per cent of students don't know what a vehicle connection is.
- Only 15% of the students were able to explain the difference between an electrical diagram and an electrical circuit.
- 80% of the students were able to define the meaning of the electrical lines in the circuit.

<u>Using the software</u>

-   80% of the students knew the meaning of grounding and the difference between a circuit and a wiring diagram.

Question 4 - Interpreting the electrical diagram

We investigated whether the students know how to interpret electrical diagrams of a lighting system circuit.

<u>Without using the *software*</u>

Regarding the diagram shown in figure 5.6, 80 per cent of the students were unable to answer what the electrical diagram was about.

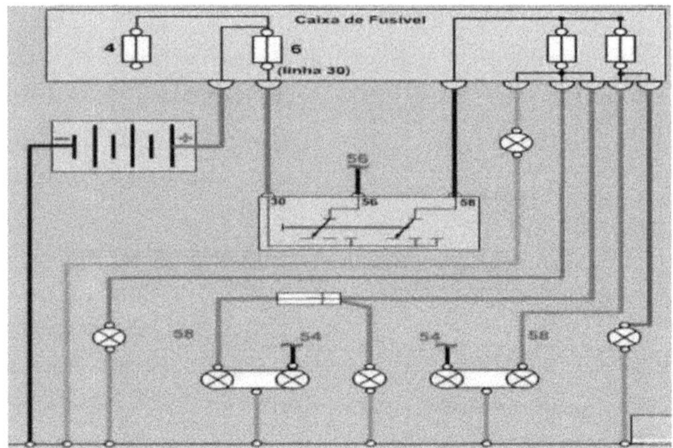

Figure 5.6: Electrical diagram 1

<u>Using the *software*</u>
The students got 100 per cent right.
Question 5 - The diagram in figure 5.7, highlighted in the assessment, was to find out what type of circuit and its purpose in the car's electrical system.

<u>Without using the *software*</u>
The result: nobody got it right about the importance of the circuit and what it's used for in the car.

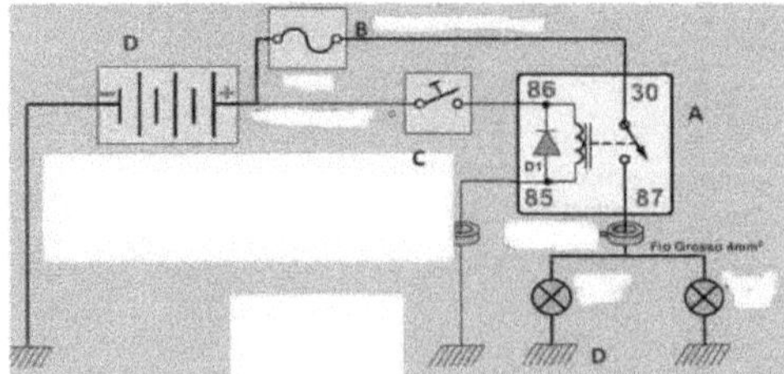

Figure 5.7: Electrical diagram with relay.

<u>Using the software</u>

40

The students who had doubts about the two lighting circuits in the first assessment, with the use of the software, improved their knowledge, bringing the number of correct diagrams to 80 per cent.

<u>Without using the software</u>

Question 6 - Another aspect in the context of interpreting electrical diagrams was to draw a parallel between figures 5.8 and 5.9 and show if there is any difference.

Figura A

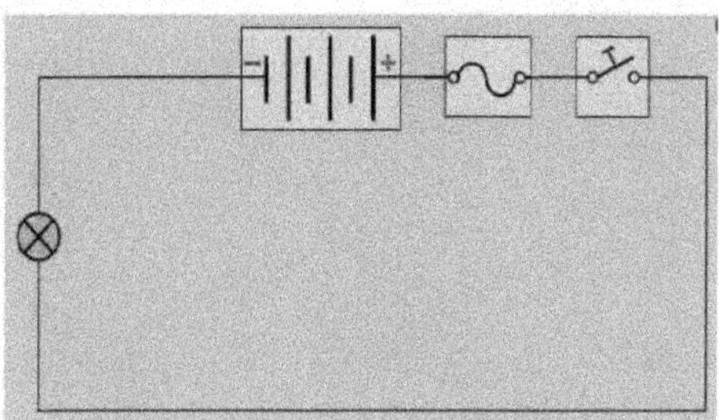

Figure 5.8: Simple circuits.

Figura B

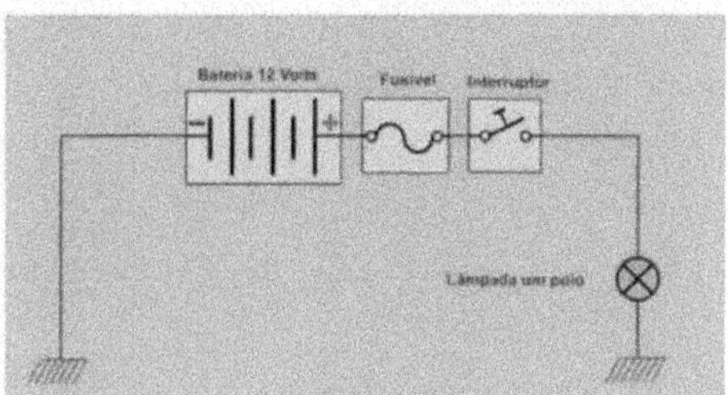

Figure 5.9: Grounding circuit.

Only one student argued his answer logically. The others left answers blank because they had no idea what the answer was.

<u>Using the *software*</u>

The next time round, there were 100 per cent correct answers, with good arguments from some students and detailed explanations.

<u>Without using the *software*</u>

Question 7 - In the last question, the vehicle headlight electrical diagram was highlighted and a few questions were asked to see if the student knew how to interpret the diagram.

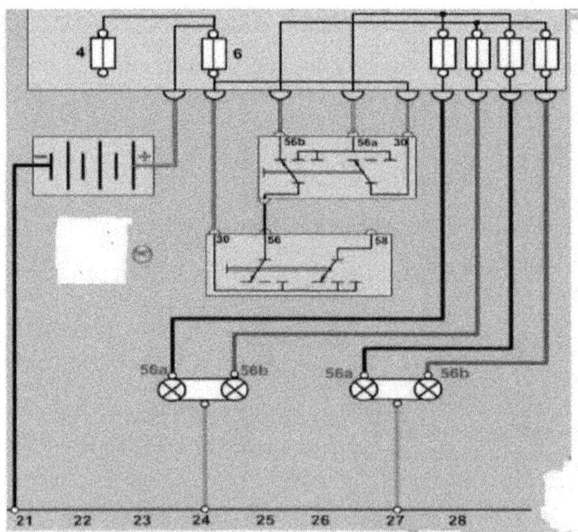

Figure 5.10: Headlamp circuit.

- 80% don't know what the wiring diagram refers to.

- 70 per cent can't tell the difference between a ground connection and a circuit.

- 75 per cent don't know the purpose of the fuse in the circuit.

Using the software

- 80% answered what the circuit was about.

- 100 % of the students were able to differentiate between a mass connection and a mass.

- 80% of students can identify the components symbolically.

- Everyone knows how to locate a fuse and check the diagram to see what it protects.

5.3   Comments on the Evaluated Results

Analysing the results of the assessment in the two PRONATEC classes, in terms of specific knowledge between class "A" and class "B", it can be concluded that the results of class "A", which used the ELTROAUTOS *software*, were very satisfactory, showing good performance in getting the proposed questions right compared to class "B".

Below are some of the aspects highlighted in class "A":

- 80% correct on all the questions proposed in the assessment.

- Good student motivation in the study of electrical circuits, using the didactic resource in the computer lab.
- Knowledge of the main symbols for car electrical components.
- They know how to distinguish between series-parallel circuits and those specific to the lighting system.
- They clearly define the meaning of grounding and automotive electrical lines.

The students in class "B", in which the *software* was not applied, showed a very low level of knowledge. This will certainly have an impact on the profession in the market, as there will be no progress due to a lack of basic and specific knowledge.

Next, we collected some relevant aspects to highlight in class "B":

- Results below the desired average, with a percentage of less than 50 per cent.
- Students don't know the main electrical symbols in the circuit.
- They don't know how to distinguish fundamental electrical circuits.
- They don't recognise the car's specific circuit in the wiring diagram.
- They have difficulty defining the connection to the ground and don't recognise it on the wiring diagram.

Certainly, if the programme had been applied in class "B", there could have been an improvement in learning in various aspects, both in terms of stimulating the students and in the approach to the content, with the use of the virtual laboratory and practical activities in the workshop, as was done in class "A".

When analysing the results in terms of interpreting the electrical diagrams, in class "A" they answered all the questions in the electrical diagram assessment, showing that the ELETROAUTOS *software* was important and decisive for learning. Once students are able to interpret a wiring diagram, they look forward to learning other, more complex car diagrams.

Class B's result in interpreting the electrical diagram was below average. This shows that the students haven't learnt much about automotive electricity.

Below are the important points to highlight about classes "A" and "B" in the process of interpreting an automotive wiring diagram:

Class "A"
- The students knew the main symbolic representations of the electrical diagram.
- The majority recognised the evaluation's wiring diagram.
- Recognise the main energised power lines.
- Recognise grounding strategies, locating them on the electrical diagram.
- They define the electrical protections, locating them on the wiring diagram.

Class "B"
- Most people don't recognise the name of the wiring diagram.
- Most students don't know how to locate the mass points on the diagram.
- Most of the electrical symbols the students don't know how to define.

- Some left blank points in their evaluation answers.

In the car maintenance apprenticeship class at the dealership Volkswagen, the students did not perform well before applying the software in some criteria.

Here are a few aspects that left something to be desired:

- 90% of students know how to define the electrical lines in a circuit.
- 80% of the students don't know the meaning of the connection to the mass and the

  difference between circuit and wiring diagram
- Only one student made a logical argument for his answer, while the others left their answers blank because they had no idea.

When the ELETROAUTOS programme was used, there was a very significant improvement in the students' learning. These aspects show how the software favoured contributing to the students' knowledge.

Here are some aspects of this improvement:

- The students who had doubts about the two lighting circuits in the first assessment using the software improved their knowledge, increasing their diagram accuracy rate to 80 per cent.
- 80% of the students were able to answer the meaning of grounding and the difference between a

  circuit and a wiring diagram.
- There was 100 per cent accuracy in identifying the fundamental circuits.
- The next time round, there were 100 per cent correct answers, with good arguments from some students, explaining in detail.

5.4   Student reports on the ELETROAUTOS software.

The students' opinions on ELETROAUTOS were collected through an interview (Appendix B). The interview consisted of eight questions, with the

The aim was to address some important aspects of the software. The interviewees have been given fictitious names when quoted in this research paper.

In terms of the ELETROAUTOS software's non-functional requirements, the interviewees' comments show that they are satisfied with some of the requirements.

The functionality of the programme, such as images, colours, illustrations and resources, was highlighted by the students.

> **"The** *images, models and colours of each part, tool and driver are well illustrated" (Abrãao).*
>
> *"The material is well illustrated and easy to understand" (Israel).*
>
> *"It explains some parts of the automotive electrical system very well" (José).*
>
> *"The programme has a feature where hovering the mouse over an abbreviation tells you the meaning" (Josué).*

Usability is another requirement highlighted by the students when using the educational software. In this respect, the students found it easy to control the programme and choose what they wanted to study from the programme's content.

> *"The programme offers a start menu that allows the **user** to choose the subject" (Davi).*

> *"The material allows us to build the circuit in the right way"* **(Samuel).**

> *"The programme's interface is very dynamic and easy" (Jecé).*

> *"The 'point and click' feature makes it easy to move through the menus"* **(Salomão).**

> *"It's* **a quick-to-learn programme that makes it easier to control** *tasks" (Samuel).*

Even though the programme's table of contents (Figure 5.4) proposes a coherent learning order for the students, the programme is non-linear, as they are free to choose the electrical circuits they want to study.

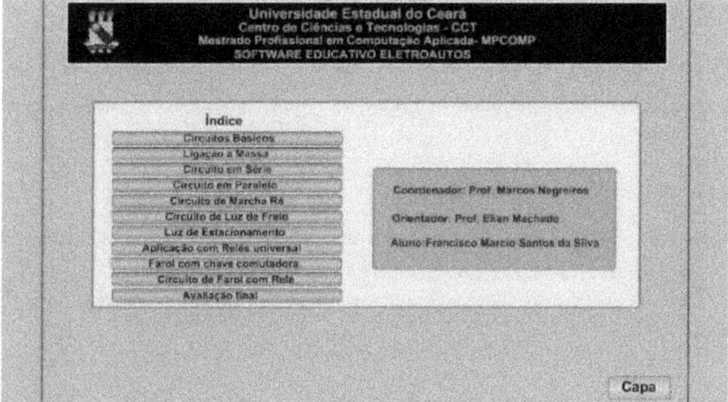

Figure 5.11: Index with circuit access order.

Content is also a criterion that was well emphasised by the interviewees. The students commented that they didn't encounter any difficulties or feel lost in their learning because they didn't understand the text.

> "The *programme has explanatory texts" (Job).*

> *"As well as easy language, some objects come with extra details if you click on them" (Zacarias).*

> *"On more specific subjects, there was content available"* **(Jabez).**

The programme holds the student's attention. Many highlighted the virtual laboratory (Figure 5.4.1) as a way of attracting attention because of the construction of electrical circuits.

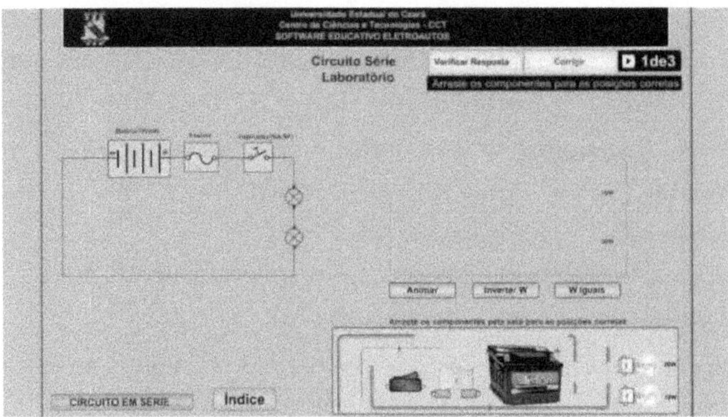

Figure 5.12: Virtual laboratory.

For the interviewees, doing the circuits is a challenge and requires concentration.

"To assemble the circuits requires attention from the user" **(Habakkuk).**

"You need to pay as much attention as possible, otherwise you might get the question wrong" **(Malachi).**

"I was very focused on the programme" **(Daniel).**

In the students' reactions, they want to develop electrical circuits other than the exercises already proposed by the programme.

5.5   Teachers analyse the software

Four teachers were interviewed and the aspects of teaching practice with the ELETROAUTOS software were analysed. Their names are also fictitious.

The teachers agreed with the idea that the software brought a better way of teaching, through its usability and user-friendly interface.

"With its interactivity and dynamism, the software facilitates the **teaching-learning** *process* **because it shows the main components of electrical systems in an easy and friendly way, as well as how they work, which without the use of the software would require a lot of abstraction on the part of the** *students" (Professor* **Raimundo).**

Professor Raimundo's comment shows that the software fulfils the expectations of electrical circuit classes. The resources have made it easier for students to think and have reduced their cognitive load.

With the teacher's next argument, we can see that the resource has been approved in electricity theory classes through the behaviour of the animations, which translate a real moment.

"The software's animations make it possible to **streamline the administration of this content, improving the assimilation of theoretical lessons as well as** *helping with practical activities"* **(Professor Paulo).**

Another important aspect is the standardisation of teaching resources. Using the software makes the technical language standardised for the students. Professor Lucas comments on this aspect:

"It favours the student and the teacher, facilitates the solution of doubts and standardises learning.

With regard to the activity with students criterion, the teachers agreed that the software could be used in an individual or collective activity. The teacher highlights the fact that using the programme in a group favoured integration with the students who began to build the electrical circuits.

"Using the *software in the laboratory allows students to interact with the circuits in question, providing them with a pedagogical experience that facilitates learning" (Professor Mateus).*

The resource gives the teacher less use of voice and repetition when explaining the content, but requires more management of teaching activities. Professor Raimundo makes a statement about using the programme to explain content:

"The *teacher will work less because the electrical diagrams are presented in a way that makes it easier for the students to visualise them, facilitating learning, not to mention the dynamism it provides by showing how the systems work.*

The programme, according to the teacher's argument, provides this pedagogical support, reflecting on his or her teaching practice, improving the didactic resources in the classroom and giving the student responsibility for learning through educational *software.*

Teachers also believe that using the *software* has a pleasant demeanour and attracts the student's attention. This keeps them motivated throughout the lesson, ensuring that they get the most out of it.

In motivation, the students' reactions are observed by the teacher, who can see their satisfaction. The following arguments, from two teachers, state this motivation in using the *software:*

"The students are happy to be able to make the electrical circuit after understanding how it works, and this is very gratifying for the teacher, as it is a sign that the student has really learnt and that the software has really facilitated the student's learning" (Lucas).

In the teachers' suggestions for improvement to the educational *software* studied, it is important to highlight the involvement of more automotive electrical circuits to continue this work, given that the programme is the start of a good idea for other automotive training programmes.

Concluding the process of researching this work among teachers, they were asked to highlight the strengths and weaknesses of the *software* analysed. The interviewees had many positive comments.

One of the strong aspects highlighted was the students' motivation, which increased when they realised that the programme was in context with what they had seen and learned in the lectures and practical explanations during the course.

Interactivity was something that added up well, especially when in the virtual laboratory there was the development of electrical circuits compatible with electrical schematics and practical activities. Professor Paulo makes an important observation:

"One of the most important points is undoubtedly the dynamic presentation of the operation of the lighting and signalling systems, the path from start to finish of the electric current. The operation of the switches, relays, ignition switches, not to mention the quality and contextualisation of the reality of the component figure where, from the pleasant experience of studying the software, the student will easily carry out the operations and interventions on the car."

Overall, the programme left a good impression on the students and teachers, as it linked the practical activities of the electricity course with the virtual laboratory.

CHAPTER 6

CONCLUSION

In this research project, a survey was carried out on vocational education and educational information technology, looking at aspects of the training of automotive mechanics. The types of vocational education and the current laws that regulate them were discussed. We looked at some educational programmes that some teachers use in their classes, but the more specific automotive electrical resources are the property of the car manufacturer, making it difficult to use the resource in other classes and learning situations.

Vocational education was emphasised, such as the PRONATEC project and the CAI course. These projects were the research laboratory for the ELETROAUTOS software, in which the entire analysis of the proposed didactic resource was carried out.

The work also included information from computer science, focusing on pedagogical usability issues, the attributes and quality of software and other important aspects of a good EDR. These elements guided the construction of the ELETROAUTOS software, which took care to incorporate good navigability and ease of use.

The aim of the research was to develop and evaluate educational software that would help students to develop knowledge of fundamental and specific electrical circuits in the automotive sector. The interviewees were directly involved in the teaching process, developing the software's content and electrical circuits, and the teachers became aware of the importance of computers and educational software in the teaching and learning process.

In the software's virtual environment, the teacher's pedagogical practice was supported, as he managed the students' activities, guiding the philosophy of the SENAI institution itself with other pedagogical resources, which has technicist hallmarks with the competency-based methodology.

The virtual laboratory gave students the opportunity to build electrical circuits without the need for wires and tools, individualising their learning by using the software at home. The teacher's role in the process was fundamental in carrying out the activities with the educational software and answering any questions that arose.

Once all the work on the ELETROAUTOS software had been carried out, the results achieved using the programme were identified. The main important aspects stand out:

a) Provided an automotive electricity resource based on car-specific electrical circuits.

b) It proposed learning automotive electricity with greater student interactivity through computer mediation.

c) It has reduced the cost of consumables in practical classes, provided by a virtual laboratory before the electrical circuit construction practicals are carried out.

d) I brought autonomous activities into the classroom for the students.

e) It provided a teaching resource for the teacher in lectures and other learning moments.

f) It facilitated the car manufacturer's specific technical language into an accessible, playful language with a light cognitive load, using computer resources.

g) It raised awareness and broke the paradigm of the traditional resources used by teachers to teach automotive electrical circuits.

During the application of the ELETROAUTOS software, there were some interesting adjustments suggested by teachers and students to improve the educational resource.

The items below are recommendations for future work:

a) Convert the ELETROAUTOS programme to the Android operating system.

b) Develop a tutorial to show the best way to use the resource in classroom and distance learning classes.

c) Develop more electrical circuits for the lighting and signalling system, using other strategies in the virtual laboratory to assemble the electrical circuits.

d) Develop other educational programmes in the automotive field, based on the essence of ELETROAUTOS.

e) Make the software available in educational repositories on the internet.

f) Develop other educational resources based on ELETROAUTOS in other programmes, such as Java or PHP.

g) Include the option to save the activities carried out by the students.

h) Allow chat interaction between students.

A test of the tool's effectiveness was carried out using three electricity classes to measure the importance of the software in shaping knowledge of electrical circuits.

As was seen in one class that didn't use the software, it was realised that many of the students had difficulty interpreting automotive electrical diagrams and that some teachers are resistant to new teaching resources and still use traditional resources and methods. Using the ELETROAUTOS software proved that the resource facilitated the students' learning and helped the teacher as a didactic tool in his practice.

The use of computer resources at school is very important, as it contributes significantly to the teaching and learning of teachers and students. The computer lab was a new environment for the theory lessons on automotive electricity. The laptops in the workshop, with the ELETROAUTOS programme to help with students' doubts about certain electrical circuits, was something new in the practical activities for learning electrical circuits.

It is hoped that the programme will be used in all forms of automotive electrical education and by all vocational education institutions, and that this resource will inspire others, forming a collection of teaching resources that will provide the automotive vocational education community with a multiplier of knowledge and the training of professionals par excellence.

REFERENCES

ANFAVEA - ASSOCIAÇÃO NACIONAL DOS FABRICANTES DE VEICULOS AUTOMOTORES.Disponível: http://www.anfavea.com.br/tabelas2009/autoveiculos/tab ela07 producao.pdf(2010). Accessed on: 24 March 2010.

BRAZILIAN ASSOCIATION OF TECHNICAL STANDARDS. NBR ISO/IEC 9126-1 - **Software engineering** - Product quality - Part 1: Quality model. São Paulo: Brazilian Association of Technical Standards - ABNT, 2003.

BRAZIL, Ministry of Education. **Guidelines and Bases Legislation**. Law No. 9.394, 19 December 2000. Access: http://www.planalto.gov.br/ccivil_03/leis/L10097.htm.

BRAZIL, Ministry of Education. **Guidelines and Bases Legislation**. Law No. 11.741, of 16 July 2008. Access: http://www.planalto.gov.br/ccivil 23/06/2012.

BRAZIL, Ministry of Education. **Guidelines and Bases Legislation**. Law No. 12.513, of 26 October 2011. Access: http://www.planalto.gov.br/ccivil 23/06/2012

BRAZIL, Ministry of Education. **Guidelines and Bases Legislation**. Law No. 10.097, of 20 December 1996. Access: http://www.planalto.gov.br/ccivil_03/Leis/L9394.htm 23/06/2012

CNI-SENAI. Automotive. **Car maintenance mechanic.** National Curriculum Design. Vol. 1, Number 1, Brasília, 2010.

CNI, SESI, SENAI. **Education for the new industry**. National Confederation of Industry. Brasilia, 2007

DELGADO, Paulo Roberto; KURESKI, Ricardo. The importance of the service sector in the state of Paraná. **Revista Paraense de Desenvolvimento**, Curitiba, n.118, p.139-158, jan./jun. 2010.

DORNELES, Pedro F.T.; ARAUJO, Ives, S.; VEIT, Eliane A. Simulação e modelagem computacionais no auxilio da aprendizagem significativa de conceitos básicos de eletricidade. **Revista Brasileira de Ensino a Física**, v. 30,n. 3, 2008, Brazil.

FERREIRA, Naidson Clayr Santos. Information technology in the teaching-learning process at the Instituto Federal Baiano - Campus Guanambi . **Informática na educação**: teoria & prática Porto Alegre, v.13, n.1, jan./jun. 2010.

FRANZONI, Gilberto; LABURÚ, Carlos Eduardo; SILVA, Osmar Henrique Moura. Drawing as a representational mediator between experiment and electrical circuit diagram. **Revista eletrônica de investigação.** Vol. 6, number 1, July 2011.
FRANCO, Maria de Fátima. Quality assessment of ELO authoring software. Texto livre linguagem e tecnologia. **Minas Gerais,** vol 4, n 2, 2006.

FRANZONI, Gilberto. LABURÚ Carlos Eduardo. SILVA Osmar Henrique Moura. Drawing as a representational mediator between experiment and electrical circuit diagram. Revista eletrônica de investigación en educación en ciencias. Volumen 6 Nro. 1. july, 2010.

IRWIN, J, David, **Introduction to electrical circuit analysis**. Ed. LTC, Auburn university, 2005.

MEURER, Zilk Herzog, STEFFANI, Maria Helena, Objeto Educacional Astronomia: ferramenta de ensino em espaços de aprendizagem formais e informais. **National Physics Symposium**, SNEF 2009, Vitória-ES.

NASCIMENTO, Adriane Suely Rodrigues do.; ARAÚJO, Ronaldo Marcos de Lima. What the articles published in the journal trabalho & educação say about training practices in vocational education. **Trabalho & Educação**, Belo Horizonte, v.19, n.1, p.53-72, jan./abr. 2010.

NOKELAINEN, Petri. An emprical assessment of pedagogical usability criteria for digital learning material with elementary school students. **Educational Technology & Society**, v. 9 (2), p. 178 - 197, 2006.

NOKELAINEN, Petri. An empirical assessment of pedagogical usability criteria for digital learning material with elementary school students. **International Forum of Educational Technology & Society IFETS**, 2006.

OLIVEIRA, Kethure Aline; AMARAL, Marília Abrahão; DOMINGOS, Gabriela Recipputi. Evaluating the use of Learning Objects in Youth and Adult Education. **Brazilian Journal of Informatics in Education**, Volume 19, Number 3, 2011.

OLIVEIRA, Camila de Oliveira. SIMÃO Leonardo Peixoto. The importance of integrating apprentices into the labour market. **Revista Faculdade Montes Belos**, v. 5, n. 1, Mar. 2012.

PEREIRA, Edvaldo da Silva. Educação de jovens e adultos-EJA e o programa de integração da educação profissional ao ensino médio na modalidade de educação de Jovens e Adultos. **Norte científico.** v.1 , n.1, December 2006.

PORTAL DO PROFESSOR. http://portaldoprofessor.mec.gov.br/index.html. Accessed 06 August 2012.

RODRIGUES et al. The importance of new technologies in the teaching and learning process. **Revista Tecer** - Belo Horizonte - vol. 1, n° 1, December 2008.

REITZ, D. S. **Evaluation of the Impact of Technical and Pedagogical Usability on Learner Performance in e-learning.** Porto Alegre: UFRS, 2009. Thesis (Doctorate) - Postgraduate Programme in Informatics in Education at the Interdisciplinary Centre for New Technologies in Education, Federal University of Rio Grande do Sul, Porto Alegre, 2009.

TAVARES, Romero. Meaningful learning, dual coding and learning objects. **Revista brasileira de informática na educação**, vol 18, n 2, 2010.

TAROUCO, Liane Margarida Rockenbach. ROLAND, Letícia Coelho. FABRE Marie- Christine Julie Mascarenhas.KONRATH, Mary Lúcia Pedroso. Educational games.

New Technologies in Education. V. 2 N° 1, March 2004. Cinted-ufrgs

VAUGHAN, Tay. **Multimedia**: Marking it work. Publisher Mc Graw ill, ed.8, 2010, New York.

WEBER, Maíra Amélia Leite. BEHRENS, Marilda Aparecida. Educational paradigms and teaching with the use of media. **Revista Intersaberes**, Curitiba, a. 5, n.10, p. 245-270, jul./dez. 2010.

APPENDIX A - Initial evaluation questionnaire

Questionnaire evaluating the educational tool ELETROAUTOS Class: Automotive maintenance apprenticeship 2012

Student: ____

1. When I work on this task I feel that I, not the programme, have control over the responsibility for my learning.

Criterion: STUDENT CONTROL

Answer:

( ) Totally agree ( ) Partially agree ( ) Undecided ( ) Partially disagree ( ) Totally disagree

7. I got so deep into this learning material that I forgot everything that was going on around me and how much time had passed.

Criterion: STUDENT ACTIVITY

( ) Totally agree ( ) Partially agree ( ) Undecided ( ) Partially disagree ( ) Totally disagree

10   . I am proud of my solutions or a solution realised with others to the problem presented in the learning material. (Definition: I feel that I or we have done something significant).

Criterion: STUDENT ACTIVITY

( ) Totally agree ( ) Partially agree ( ) Undecided ( ) Partially disagree ( ) Totally disagree

11   This learning material lets me talk to my colleagues.

Criterion: COOPERATIVE/COLLABORATIVE LEARNING

( ) Totally agree ( ) Partially agree ( ) Undecided ( ) Partially disagree ( ) Totally disagree

13. It's nice to use the learning material with another student on the same computer.

Criterion: COOPERATIVE/COLLABORATIVE LEARNING, MOTIVATION

( ) Totally agree ( ) Partially agree ( ) Undecided ( ) Partially disagree ( ) Totally disagree

20.   This learning material clearly tells me what I'm expecting to know (or learn) after I've used it Criterion: OBJECTIVE ORIENTATION

( ) Totally agree ( ) Partially agree ( ) Undecided ( ) Partially disagree ( ) Totally disagree

21.   This learning material clearly shows why it is useful to learn it. (Definition: Learning objectives are justified, e.g. "This task will help you to make interrogative sentences in the English language"). Criterion: OBJECTIVE ORIENTATION

( ) Totally agree ( ) Partially agree ( ) Undecided ( ) Partially disagree ( ) Totally disagree

23.   This learning material shows how much progress I've made in my studies (Definition: I know what I've learnt or I have to learn more).

Criterion: GOAL ORIENTATION

( ) Totally agree ( ) Partially agree ( ) Undecided ( ) Partially disagree ( ) Totally disagree

26.   I feel that I am able to use the skills and knowledge that this learning material has taught me in the future.

Criterion: APPLICABILITY

( ) Totally agree ( ) Partially agree ( ) Undecided ( ) Partially disagree ( ) Totally disagree

29.   This learning material is adequately challenging for me. (Definition: The tasks are not so easy or so difficult).

Criterion: APPLICABILITY

( ) Totally agree ( ) Partially agree ( ) Undecided ( ) Partially disagree ( ) Totally disagree

32. The images and sounds in this learning material help you learn.

Criterion: ADDED VALUE

( ) Totally agree ( ) Partially agree ( ) Undecided ( ) Partially disagree ( ) Totally disagree

35. It is more useful to learn topics with this learning material than with conventional methods in a classroom. (Definition: Think about whether you would be more willing to do these tasks with a computer or with a normal study book or exercise book).

Criterion: ADDED VALUE

( ) Totally agree ( ) Partially agree ( ) Undecided ( ) Partially disagree ( ) Totally disagree

38.   I'm interested in the topics in this learning material.

Criterion: MOTIVATION

( ) Totally agree ( ) Partially agree ( ) Undecided ( ) Partially disagree ( ) Totally disagree

39.   This learning material requires me to know something that has been thought of in some other learning material. (Definition: This material refers to some other learning material).

Criterion: EVALUATION OF PRIOR KNOWLEDGE

( ) Totally agree ( ) Partially agree ( ) Undecided ( ) Partially disagree ( ) Totally disagree

41.   This learning material reviews previous materials before starting to teach a new topic. (Definition: For example, in maths, the material first starts with simple calculations that are needed to learn a more difficult topic).

Criterion: EVALUATION OF PRIOR KNOWLEDGE

( ) Totally agree ( ) Partially agree ( ) Undecided ( ) Partially disagree ( ) Totally disagree

42.   This learning material offers optional paths for my progress (Definition: I can choose different tasks each time I use the system).

Criterion: FLEXIBILITY

( ) Totally agree ( ) Partially agree ( ) Undecided ( ) Partially disagree ( ) Totally disagree

45.   This learning material makes it quick and easy to learn a new topic or recap on a previous one.

Criterion: ADDED VALUE

( ) Totally agree ( ) Partially agree ( ) Undecided ( ) Partially disagree ( ) Totally disagree

48.   This learning material presents information in a format that makes it easy to learn. (Definition: The information is presented in a meaningful and interconnected way and not in separate parts that are difficult to understand).

Criteria: STUDENT CONTROL, APPLICABILITY

( ) Totally agree ( ) Partially agree ( ) Undecided ( ) Partially disagree ( ) Totally disagree

51.   When I make a mistake in solving a task, the programme sends me a friendly warning.

Criterion: FEEDBACK

( ) Totally agree ( ) Partially agree ( ) Undecided ( ) Partially disagree ( ) Totally disagree

52.   This learning material gives me motivating feedback. (Definition: I want to test the less used functions in the learning material because I know it will give me all the feedback I need).

Criterion: FEEDBACK

( ) Totally agree ( ) Partially agree ( ) Undecided ( ) Partially disagree ( ) Totally disagree

56.   I think I learn more quickly with this material than I normally do. (Definition: This learning material provides the right kind of support when I need it).

Criterion: APPLICABILITY

( ) Totally agree ( ) Partially agree ( ) Undecided ( ) Partially disagree   ( )   Disagree
                    totally

APPENDIX B - Interview with the students

Class: Automotive maintenance apprenticeship

Student:____

Hello, mate!

The questions in this questionnaire are designed to assess the user-friendliness of the software you have just used. Please feel free to answer, as it is this material that is being evaluated, not you.

1.   How well can you visualise the resources available in this material?
____
____
____
____

2.   Can you easily understand the words, names, abbreviations or symbols in this material?
____
____
____
____

3. Does it allow you to easily switch between menus or screens?

____

____

____

4. Can this material be understood and used by any student, with little or a lot of experience in using computers?

____

____

____

5. Was it easy to learn how to use it? Didn't you have to ask the teacher for a lot of help until you understood how the system worked?

____

____

____

6. Do you think the content of this material keeps your attention?

____

____

____

7. Do you feel you have control over the tasks you do? (The system doesn't just make you go from one step to the next, you have control over the order in which you complete your tasks)

____

____

____

8. Have you found any limitations in this material? Don't you have an extra tip or information for any doubt or curiosity?

APPENDIX C- Interview with the Teachers

Educational software evaluation questionnaire - **ELETROAUTOS.**

Objective: To make technical and pedagogical corrections to the software.

a) TEACHING PRACTICE

1. It is a suitable resource for use in lectures on basic electricity and vehicle lighting and signalling systems.

Criteria: Lectures

Answer:

( ) Totally agree ( ) Partially agree ( ) Undecided ( ) Partially disagree ( ) Totally disagree

Opinion:

____

____

____

____

2.   This resource can be used in an individualised or group activity in the computer lab.

Criterion: Activity with students

Answer:

( ) Totally agree ( ) Partially agree ( ) Undecided ( ) Partially disagree ( ) Totally disagree

Opinion:

____

____

____

____

3.   Using this resource, the teacher works harder than using routine methods. Criterion: Teacher action

answer

( ) Totally agree ( ) Partially agree ( ) Undecided ( ) Partially disagree ( ) Totally disagree

Opinion:

____

____

____

____

4.   It is pleasant and motivating to use the software for students' learning.

Criterion: Learning and motivation.

( ) Totally agree ( ) Partially agree ( ) Undecided ( ) Partially disagree ( ) Totally disagree.

Opinion:

____

____

____

____

____

____

____

5.   In terms of teaching using the ELETROAUTOS software, what suggestions could you make to improve the resource?

Opinion:

____

6. What are the strengths of the resource for student learning?

8) Technical aspects

Evaluate the circuits by ticking X in the **AGREE** column in the table if you agree, and X in the **SUGGEST** column if you have any suggestions. In the case of a suggestion, you should give your opinion on the corresponding number of the circuit below.

1. Basic circuit
2. Mass connection
3. Series connection
4. Parallel connection
5. Reverse circuit
6. Brake light circuit

7. Parking light
8. Application with universal relays
9. Headlamp with toggle switch
10. Headlamp circuit with relay

Table I

Item	Circuit	I AGREE	SUGGEST
1	Basic circuit		
2	Mass connection		
3	Series connection		
4	Parallel connection		
5	Reverse circuit		
6	Brake light circuit		
7	Parking light		
8	Application with universal relay		
9	Headlamp with toggle switch		
10	Headlamp circuit with relay		

1. Basic circuit

2. Mass connection

2.   Series connection

3.   Parallel connection

4.   Reverse circuit

5.   Brake light circuit

6.   Parking light

7.   Application with universal relays

8.   Headlamp with toggle switch

11. Headlamp circuit with relay

APPENDIX D - Evaluation of learning progress

SENAI - NATIONAL INDUSTRIAL LEARNING SERVICE

KNOWLEDGE TEST - AUTOMOTIVE ELECTRICAL CIRCUITS

PARTICIPANT : ____

COURSE : ____

1. ABOUT THE BASIC CIRCUIT LIST EACH CIRCUIT FIGURE IN THE RECTANGLE ACCORDING TO THE NUMBERING OF THE COMPONENTS BELOW.

    1. Battery
    2. Light bulb
    3. Switch
    4. Fuse

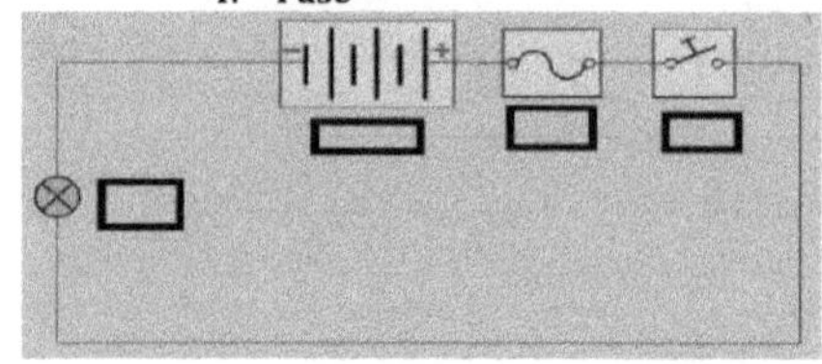

2. ASSOCIATE THE SYMBOLS WITH THE NAMES OF THE COMPONENTS REPRESENTED BELOW

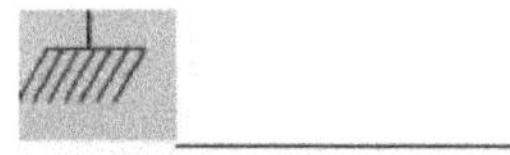 _______________

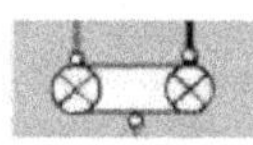 _______________

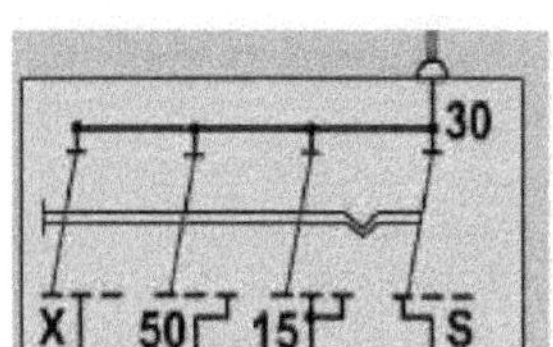

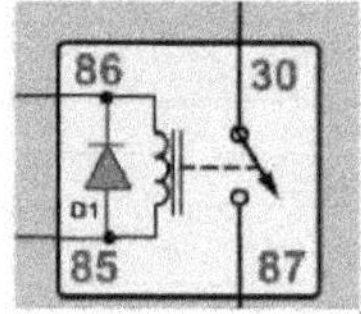 _______________

____

3. LOOKING AT THE FIGURES BELOW, LIST WHICH IS THE SERIES CIRCUIT AND WHICH IS THE SERIES CIRCUIT.

PARALLEL.
a) Circuit _______________________________________

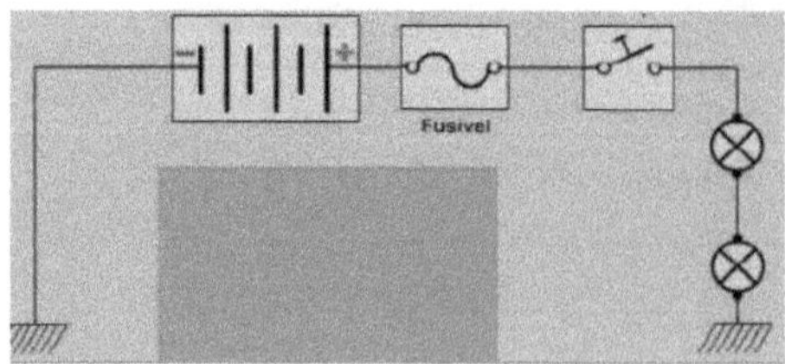

B) Circuit _______________________________________

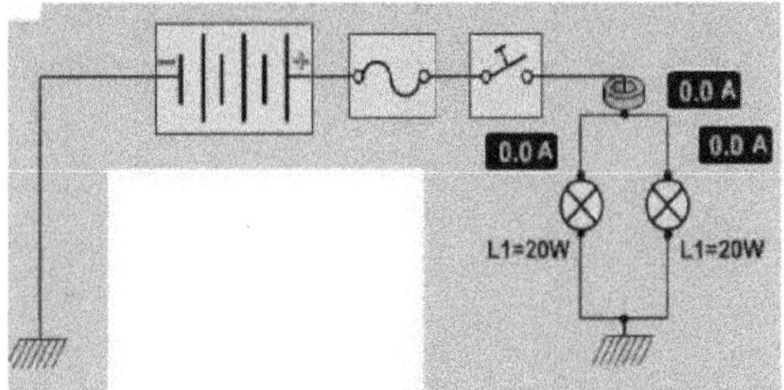

4. WHAT YOU MEAN BY GROUNDING IN VEHICLE ELECTRICITY

____

____

____

____

5. DIFFERENTIATE BETWEEN AN ELECTRICAL DIAGRAM AND AN ELECTRICAL CIRCUIT.

____

____

____

6. WHAT IS THE NAME OF THE CIRCUIT BELOW?

7. RELATE THE FIRST COLUMN TO THE SECOND.

(A) Parking light	( ) Line 56
(B) Direct from the battery	( ) Line 15
(C) Ignition	( ) Line 58
(D) Lighthouse	( ) Line 30
(E) Accessories	( ) Line X
(F) Mass	( ) Line 31

8. ANSWER THE QUESTION BASED ON THE DRAWING BELOW

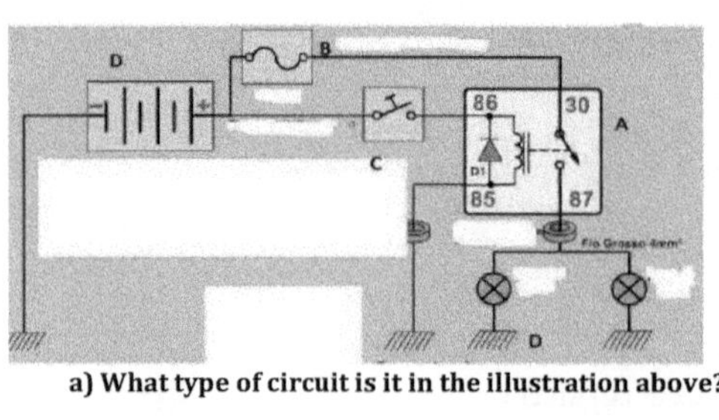

a) What type of circuit is it in the illustration above?

____

____

____

____

b) What do the components associated with the letters A, B, C, D stand for?

____

____

____

____

9) LOOKING AT THE ELECTRICAL DIAGRAMS BELOW, ANSWER THE QUESTION BELOW. Circuit A

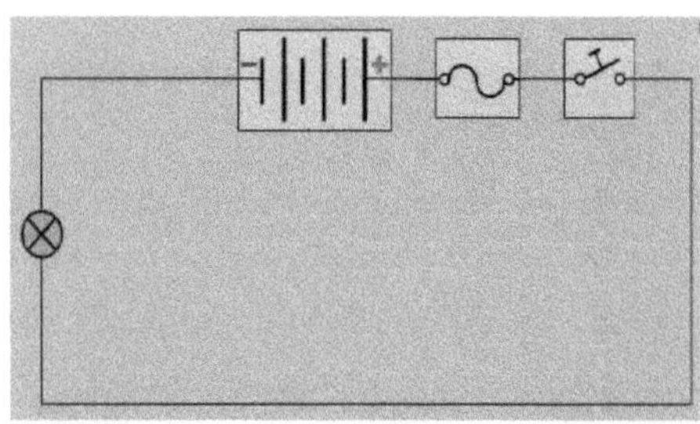

Circuit B

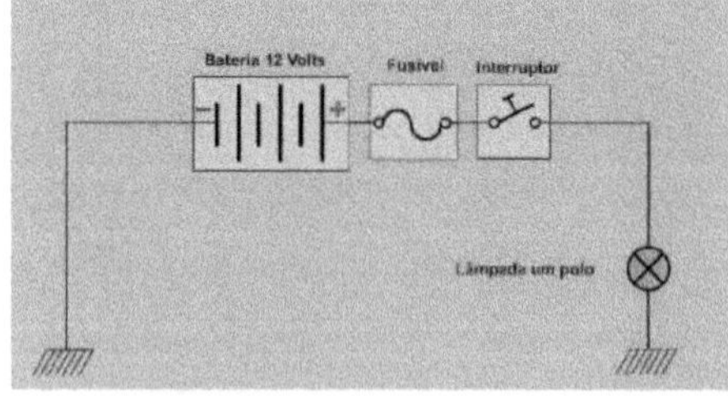

A) Is there any difference between the two electrical diagrams? Justify your answer.

____

____

____

1) ELECTRICAL CIRCUIT INTERPRETATION

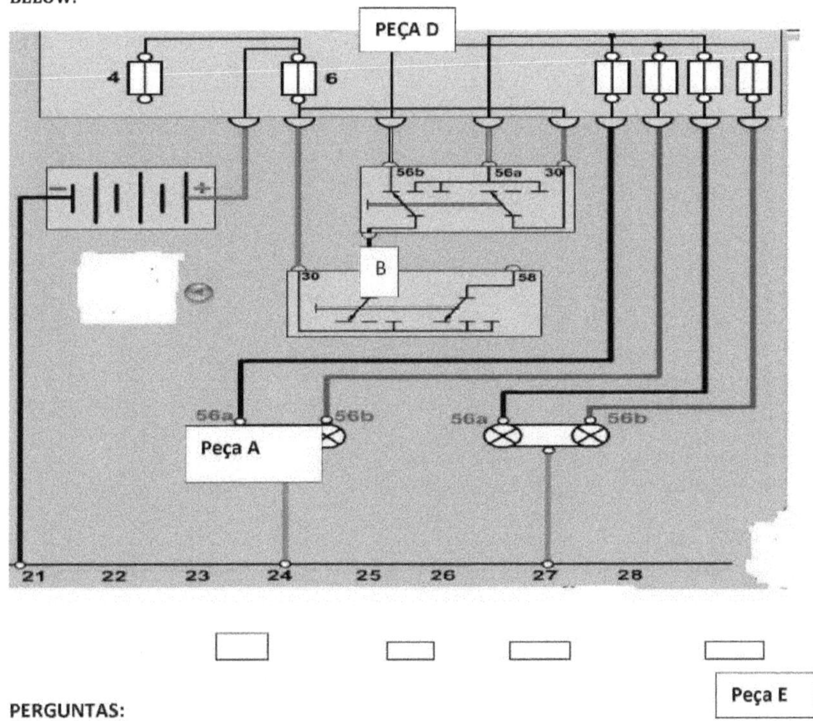

PERGUNTAS:

1) What type of electrical circuit is in the diagram?

2) Which power line feeds this circuit.

3) What does **line 27** below the circuit mean

4) What is **Part A** in the circuit?

5) **Fuse 4** supplies which part of the circuit.

6) What is the name of **part B**?

7) What is the name of **part D?**

8) What is the meaning of the **number 21** in the line below the circuit?

9) What is the name of the **piece?**

10) What happens when I cut the wire that connects to the **number 21**?